New Wave English Skills Practice

E

Revised edition

This book belongs to:

New wave English skills practice *(Book E)*

Published by R.I.C. Publications® 2014

Revised and reprinted 2022
Reprinted 2023, 2024, 2025
ISBN 978-1-922843-58-6
RIC–6224

Titles available in this series:
New wave English skills practice *(Book A)*
New wave English skills practice *(Book B)*
New wave English skills practice *(Book C)*
New wave English skills practice *(Book D)*
New wave English skills practice *(Book E)*
New wave English skills practice *(Book F)*

R.I.C. Publications® follows the guidelines for punctuation and grammar as recommended by the *Style manual for authors, editors and printers*, 2002, 6th edn.

Note, however, that teachers should use their own guide if there is a conflict.

R.I.C. Publications® acknowledges the Wadjak people of the Nyoongar Nation as the Traditional Custodians of the land on which our Western Australian office is based. We acknowledge the Traditional Custodians of Country throughout Australia and pay our respects to Elders past and present. R.I.C. Publications® recognises the role of First Nations Elders as Australia's first educators.

R.I.C. Publications®

PO Box 332
Greenwood
Western Australia 6924
+61 8 9240 9888
ricpublications.com.au
mail@ricpublications.com.au

FOREWORD

In this daily practice workbook you will be able to develop your ability to use English. Each day, you will have questions to answer in the areas of spelling, word study, punctuation and grammar. There are 160 days of questions in this workbook.

Seven weeks of each unit begin with a new skill focus. This will help remind you of some of the skills and terminology that will be used throughout the workbook. Every day, two questions will focus on the skill that is introduced at the start of the week. The remaining questions will be mixed practice which will help to improve your English skills as well as your knowledge about how language works.

At the completion of each unit, you will have the opportunity to review what you have learnt by doing one day of skill focus revision questions. Your daily scores are recorded in the bubble at the bottom of each day. These daily scores can be transferred onto the record sheets at the front of your book.

This will give an overview of your performance for the whole school year. Be sure to read each question carefully before you answer it. If you find a question too difficult, move on to the next one. If you have time at the end, you can go back to the one you haven't done.

CONTENTS

Record sheet

Week 1		Week 2		Week 3		Week 4	
Date		*Date*		*Date*		*Date*	
Skill focus		Skill focus		Skill focus		Skill focus	
Day 1		Day 1		Day 1		Day 1	
Day 2		Day 2		Day 2		Day 2	
Day 3		Day 3		Day 3		Day 3	
Day 4		Day 4		Day 4		Day 4	
Day 5		Day 5		Day 5		Day 5	

Week 5		Week 6		Week 7		Week 8	
Date		*Date*		*Date*		*Date*	
Skill focus		Skill focus		Skill focus		Day 1	
Day 1		Day 1		Day 1		Day 2	
Day 2		Day 2		Day 2		Day 3	
Day 3		Day 3		Day 3		Day 4	
Day 4		Day 4		Day 4		Day 5	
Day 5		Day 5		Day 5		Revision	

Week 9		Week 10		Week 11		Week 12	
Date		*Date*		*Date*		*Date*	
Skill focus		Skill focus		Skill focus		Skill focus	
Day 1		Day 1		Day 1		Day 1	
Day 2		Day 2		Day 2		Day 2	
Day 3		Day 3		Day 3		Day 3	
Day 4		Day 4		Day 4		Day 4	
Day 5		Day 5		Day 5		Day 5	

Week 13		Week 14		Week 15		Week 16	
Date		*Date*		*Date*		*Date*	
Skill focus		Skill focus		Skill focus		Day 1	
Day 1		Day 1		Day 1		Day 2	
Day 2		Day 2		Day 2		Day 3	
Day 3		Day 3		Day 3		Day 4	
Day 4		Day 4		Day 4		Day 5	
Day 5		Day 5		Day 5		Revision	

Record sheet

Week 17		Week 18		Week 19		Week 20	
Date		*Date*		*Date*		*Date*	
Skill focus		Skill focus		Skill focus		Skill focus	
Day 1		Day 1		Day 1		Day 1	
Day 2		Day 2		Day 2		Day 2	
Day 3		Day 3		Day 3		Day 3	
Day 4		Day 4		Day 4		Day 4	
Day 5		Day 5		Day 5		Day 5	

Week 21		Week 22		Week 23		Week 24	
Date		*Date*		*Date*		*Date*	
Skill focus		Skill focus		Skill focus		Day 1	
Day 1		Day 1		Day 1		Day 2	
Day 2		Day 2		Day 2		Day 3	
Day 3		Day 3		Day 3		Day 4	
Day 4		Day 4		Day 4		Day 5	
Day 5		Day 5		Day 5		Revision	

Week 25		Week 26		Week 27		Week 28	
Date		*Date*		*Date*		*Date*	
Skill focus		Skill focus		Skill focus		Skill focus	
Day 1		Day 1		Day 1		Day 1	
Day 2		Day 2		Day 2		Day 2	
Day 3		Day 3		Day 3		Day 3	
Day 4		Day 4		Day 4		Day 4	
Day 5		Day 5		Day 5		Day 5	

Week 29		Week 30		Week 31		Week 32	
Date		*Date*		*Date*		*Date*	
Skill focus		Skill focus		Skill focus		Day 1	
Day 1		Day 1		Day 1		Day 2	
Day 2		Day 2		Day 2		Day 3	
Day 3		Day 3		Day 3		Day 4	
Day 4		Day 4		Day 4		Day 5	
Day 5		Day 5		Day 5		Revision	

Skill focus

Types of nouns

Nouns are important words. They are used to name people, places, things, feelings or ideas.

There are many different types of nouns. Let's learn more about four of these.

Common nouns

These are the non-specific names used for people, places and things.

doctor

mountain

building friend day

Proper nouns

Proper nouns tell us exactly who or what are the specific things in a sentence. They always start with a capital letter.

Doctor Dolittle

Mount Everest

Eiffel Tower Jenny and John Tuesday

Collective nouns

These are the names given to groups of people, places or things.

a class of children

a bouquet of flowers

a flight of stairs a herd of cattle

Abstract nouns

These are things that you can't see or touch, like feelings or ideas.

happiness

friendship

birthday

Practice questions

1. Write the type of noun that is underlined.

Sara is in <u>love</u> with her new puppy.

(a) ____________

While scuba diving, we saw a <u>school</u> of fish

(b) ____________

Jack's birthday is in <u>December</u>.

(c) ____________

Watch out for those <u>bees</u>!

(d) ____________

Day 1

1. Circle the common nouns.

   A frog inhabiting the Amazon Basin has horns and a very large mouth.

2. Circle the proper nouns.

   Some frogs living in dense, tropical forests of Borneo and Malaysia live in trees.

3. Correct the spelling mistake. ____________

   Frogs' eggs are redy to hatch in 6 to 21 days.

4. Is the underlined word a synonym (similar meaning) for ***above***? Yes ☐ No ☐

   lower <u>overhead</u> overhang

5. Add a prefix to make the words mean the opposite.

   ____employed ____natural

6. Write ***would not*** as a contraction.

   ____

7. Write the homophone for ***break***.

   ____

8. Write the plural of ***tax***.

   ____

9. Punctuate the sentence.

   young tadpoles swim around and feed on algae

10. Add a comma to the list.

    Adult frogs eat insects worms snails and spiders.

11. Add an apostrophe to show possession.
    Hint: the apostrophe's tail points to the owner.

    A frogs long, sticky tongue helps it to catch food.

12. How many nouns? ____________

    Frogs live on all continents except for Antarctica, where the climate isn't suitable.

13. Circle the conjunction.

    The amazing frogs glide smoothly and effortlessly.

14. Circle two words that describe the underlined noun.

    Male frogs use loud, croaking <u>noises</u> to attract females.

15. Circle the word that doesn't belong.

    When a tadpole hatches from the egg, it stays hiding among a water plants.

Day 2

1. Circle the collective noun.
   A cluster of stars can be seen through a telescope.
2. How many nouns? ______________
   Earth receives its warmth and light from the sun.
3. Correct the spelling mistake. ______________
   From space, Earth looks like it is made of blue matereel.
4. An antonym (opposite) for ***decrease*** is:
   lessen increase subject
5. Add a prefix to make the words mean the opposite.
   _____correct _____convenient
6. Expand the contraction ***they're***. ______________
7. Write the homophone for ***meet***. ______________
8. Write the plural of ***sheep***. ______________
9. Punctuate the sentence.
   the oceans make earth look blue
10. Add a comma to the list.
    Earth's atmosphere is composed of nitrogen oxygen argon and small amounts of other gases.
11. Add an apostrophe to show possession.
    Ocean water covers about 71% of Earths surface.
12. Circle the proper nouns.
    Carl Sagan was an American astronomer who helped with space missions to Mars.
13. Circle the conjunction.
    Astronomers have learned a lot about space, but there is much more to learn.
14. Circle two words that describe the underlined nouns.
    Wise <u>astronomers</u> have studied distant <u>planets</u> for years.
15. Is the correct noun used? Yes ☐ No ☐
    A <u>telephone</u> helps astronomers to study space but it needs to have powerful lenses.

Day 3

WEEK 1

1. Circle the common nouns.
   Did you know that all dinosaurs on Earth lived on land; none flew or lived in water.
2. Circle the proper nouns.
   The enormous Tyrannosaurus once lived in North America.
3. Write the jumbled word correctly. ______________
   Fossils can be found tebwene layers of rock.
4. A synonym (similar meaning) for ***connect*** is:
   attach break construct
5. Add a prefix to make the antonyms.
   _____obey _____honest
6. Write ***does not*** as a contraction. ______________
7. What is a homophone for ***heal***? ______________
8. What is the plural of ***shelf***? ______________
9. Punctuate the sentence.
   is a palaeontologist a scientist who studies fossils
10. Add a comma to the list.
    Fossils can be made from teeth claws or bone.
11. Add an apostrophe to show possession.
    A dinosaurs fossilised footprint can reveal many things.
12. How many nouns? ______________
    Palaeontologists study bones, teeth, footprints and nests that once belonged to dinosaurs.
13. Circle the conjunction.
    Dinosaurs had hard, blunt teeth so they could tear leaves.
14. Circle the word that describes the underlined noun.
    The class created an imaginative <u>project</u> on dinosaurs.
15. Insert a full stop and a capital letter to make two sentences.
    Dinosaurs lived on Earth more than 65 million years ago many of them were slow, heavy movers.

Day 4

1. Circle the collective noun.
   A fleet of cars was travelling through the tunnel.
2. How many nouns? ____________
   The medics and firefighters assisted a woman who was injured in an accident.
3. Correct the spelling mistake. ____________
   We counted fourty speeding vehicles on the road.
4. Circle an antonym (opposite) for ***divide***.
   divert unite separate
5. Add a prefix to make the antonyms.
   _____behave _____lead
6. Expand the contraction ***don't***. ____________
7. What is the homophone for ***hear***? ____________
8. What is the plural of ***potato***? ____________
9. Punctuate the sentence.
   the traffic on main street has greatly increased
10. Add a comma or commas.
    Vehicles include cars lorries motorcycles and vans.
11. Add an apostrophe to show possession.
    The drivers patience was tested on the busy road.
12. How many nouns? ____________
    The curious reporters gathered around the injured driver of the vehicle.
13. Is the word ***made*** a conjunction?
    Yes ☐ No ☐
    The oily, wet road made it difficult to brake.
14. Circle two words that describe the underlined nouns.
    A passenger in the car suffered deep cuts and severe bruising.
15. Choose the better word. ***concerned*** ***excited***
    An ambulance officer said she was
    ____________ *that there could have been more injuries.*

MY SCORE

Day 5

1. Circle the common nouns.
   The plane taxied to the runway as we sat comfortably in our seats.
2. Circle the proper nouns.
   We travelled by plane last December for our vacation to Italy and France.
3. Correct the spelling mistake. ____________
   Our family is travelling to Singapore in Febuary.
4. An antonym (opposite) for ***awful*** is: ____________
   awkward pleasant terrible
5. Add a prefix to make the antonyms.
   _____legal _____legible
6. Expand the contraction ***wasn't***. ____________
7. Write the homophone for ***seller***. ____________
8. Is the underlined word the plural of ***woman***?
   Yes ☐ No ☐
   womans women
9. Punctuate the sentence.
   the flight from hobart to sydney takes about two hours
10. Add a comma or commas.
    I ate my meal watched an exciting film and listened to pop songs.
11. Add an apostrophe to show possession.
    Mums bag was over the allowance.
12. Circle the abstract noun.
    My mum has a fear of flying.
13. Circle the conjunction.
    The air turbulence got stronger overnight and kept us awake.
14. Circle the word that describes the underlined noun.
    The passengers were relieved when the bumpy flight was over.
15. Insert a full stop and a capital letter to make two sentences.
    It is more comfortable to sleep with your seat back some airlines also provide pillows and blankets.

MY SCORE

Skill focus

Adjectives and noun phrases

Adjectives describe the quantity, appearance, qualities, purpose or age of a noun or pronoun.

The **old**, **slimy** frog is sitting on a lily pad.

The adjectives ***old*** and ***slimy*** describe the frog. In this sentence, the main noun (frog), a word that points to it (The) and the adjectives that describe it (old, slimy) form a **noun phrase**: *the old, slimy frog*.

Two types of adjectives are used to compare two or more things.

Comparative adjectives are used to compare two things, usually by adding the suffix ***er***.

Today is **warm** but yesterday was **warmer**.

Superlative adjectives are used to compare *more than two things*, usually by adding the suffix ***est***.

Tomorrow is expected to be the **warmest** day.

The words ***more*** and ***most*** are sometimes used before some adjectives that compare things.

That book is **more interesting** than those ones, but this is the **most interesting** book I have read.

Hint: remember the spelling rules for adding suffixes:

- Words ending in a consonant then ***y***: change ***y*** to ***i*** then add the suffix.
- Words ending in silent ***e***: drop the ***e*** then add the suffix.
- One syllable words with a short vowel followed by consonant: double final consonant then add the suffix.

Practice questions

1. Circle the adjectives.

   Finally, the energetic puppy was sleeping peacefully under a shady tree.

2. Write the comparative and superlative adjectives.

   I think puppies are cuter than kittens, but my puppy is the cutest of them all.

   ____________ ____________

3. Circle the noun phrase.

   The adorable little puppy woke up with a fright.

Day 1

WEEK 2

1. Circle the adjectives.

   The famous spy took part in secret missions and dangerous adventures.

2. Circle the superlative adjective.

   His most memorable mission was in France.

3. Write the jumbled word correctly. ____________

   It is interesting to alenr about your family history.

4. Write the synonym for ***satisfied***. ____________

   contented safe miserable

5. Add the suffix ***ing*** to ***forget***. ____________

6. Write ***I will*** as a contraction. ____________

7. What is the homophone for ***piece***? ____________

8. What is the plural of ***spy***? ____________

9. Punctuate the sentence.

   did your cousin emigrate to mexico or canada

10. Add speech marks to show what was said.
    Hint: speech marks enclose words that are said.

    Dad, do you know about our family history? I asked.

11. Add one or more apostrophes to show possession.

    'Our most unusual ancestors occupations was that of a clown!' he replied.

12. Circle the collective noun.

    A tourist was trampled on by a herd of elephants.

13. How many nouns? ____________

    The tourist was observing gorillas and lions when it happened.

14. Circle the word which does not belong.

    The incident was reported by a news programs around the world.

15. Insert an appropriate question word.

    '____________ else do you know about it?' I asked.

Day 2

1. Circle the adjectives.

   A skilful gardener can make a bonsai tree look like a miniature tree.

2. Which is correct? ***harder*** ***hardest***

   Watering a bonsai is the ____________ thing to work out.

3. Rearrange the letters to make a word that means a ***type of food***.

   irfut ____________

4. Write the synonym for ***enormous***. ____________

   extra immense tiny

5. Add the suffix ***er*** to ***begin***. ____________

6. Write ***how has*** as a contraction. ____________

7. Write the homophone for ***pail***. ____________

8. What is the singular of ***churches***?
   Hint: singular = only one.

   ____

9. Punctuate the sentence.

   the art of growing bonsai trees originated in japan

10. Add speech marks to show what was said.

    Is a bonsai tree naturally very small? I asked.

11. Add one or more apostrophes to show possession.

    'This trees leaves and branches are regularly trimmed,' explained the gardener.

12. Circle the nouns.

    The bonsai is planted in a container and needs sunlight each day.

13. Circle the proper nouns.

    The art of bonsai originated in China and later spread to Japan and Korea.

14. Circle the noun phrase.

    Bonsai trees are usually repotted every two years.

15. Insert an appropriate question word.

    '____________ often do bonsais need to be watered?' I asked the gardener.

Day 3

1. Circle the adjectives.

   A newborn elephant calf has ginger hair and thick skin.

2. Circle the superlative adjective.

   Fully grown, the elephant is the largest living land animal.

3. Correct the spelling mistake. ____________

   Allthough a rhinoceros is large, an elephant is larger.

4. Write the antonym for ***brief***. ____________

   short long narrow

5. Add the suffix ***ed*** to ***occur***. ____________

6. Write ***how is*** as a contraction. ____________

7. What is the homophone for ***through***?

   ____

8. The underlined word is plural for ***deer***.

   Yes ☐ No ☐

   deer <u>deers</u>

9. Punctuate the sentence.

   species of elephant include the african and indian

10. Add speech marks to show what was said.

    That elephant weighs 5000 kg! she exclaimed.

11. Add one or more apostrophes to show possession.

    An African elephants tusks are about three metres in length.

12. Circle the collective noun.

    As parades of elephants walk across the land, they trample plants.

13. How many nouns? ____________

    The young elephant is called a calf.

14. Circle the noun phrase.

    The oldest female elephant is in charge.

15. Insert a full stop and a capital letter to make two sentences.

    A female elephant will look after a calf this happens if its mother has died.

Day 4

1. Circle the adjectives.

   Home-made smoothies are delicious and healthy.

2. Which is correct? ***deliciouser*** ***more delicious***

   I think scrambled eggs are ______________ than smoothies.

3. Correct the spelling mistake. ______________

   Chokolate is not a healthy breakfast choice.

4. The underlined word is a synonym for ***leave***.
   Yes ☐ No ☐

   arrive depart late

5. Add the suffix ***er*** to ***travel***. ______________

6. Write ***you would*** as a contraction. ______________

7. What is the homophone for ***our***? ______________

8. What is the singular of ***copies***? ______________

9. Punctuate the sentence.

   are cereal fruit and yoghurt healthy breakfast choices

10. Add speech marks to show what was said.

    What did you spread on your toast? my sister asked.

11. Add one or more apostrophes to show possession.

    After a nights sleep, our bodies need 'refuelling'.

12. Circle the abstract noun.

    Eating a good breakfast fills us with happiness.

13. How many nouns? ______________

    On Saturdays, we have eggs or pancakes for breakfast.

14. Circle the word which does not belong.

    Dad helped Mum himself to Mum's baked beans on toast.

15. Insert an appropriate question word.

    ______________ *are some of the important reasons to eat breakfast?*

Day 5

1. Circle the adjectives.

   We awoke to the delightful sounds of chirping birds in the nearby tree.

2. Circle the comparative adjective.

   The bait we bought for fishing became smellier as the day went on.

3. Rearrange the letters to make a word that means ***simple to do***.

   syea ______________

4. Write the antonym for ***continue***. ______________

   cease remain late

5. Add the suffix ***ing*** to ***prefer***. ______________

6. Write ***who will*** as a contraction. ______________

7. Write the homophone for ***coarse***. ______________

8. What is the singular of ***people***? ______________

9. Punctuate the sentence.

   we arrived at lakeside caravan park last sunday

10. Add speech marks to show what was said.

    Let's go canoeing on the lake! yelled my brother.

11. Add one or more apostrophes to show possession.

    My brothers canoe was larger than the others.

12. Circle the collective noun.

    We saw a fleet of ships sailing into the harbour.

13. Circle the proper nouns.

    My brother Billy and I paddled our canoes under Lakeview Bridge.

14. Circle the word which does not belong.

    After lots of paddling, we had finally not arrived at our picnic spot.

15. Insert a full stop and a capital letter to make two sentences.

    Later we enjoyed a delicious dinner we prepared this in our caravan.

Skill focus

Verbs, verb groups and tense

Every sentence must include a verb. A verb is a word which shows actions, or states of being (*is, am, are*) or having (*has, have*).

Many verbs have more than one part—one or more helping verbs and a main verb. This is called a **verb group**.

Most verbs and verb groups change their form. One reason they do this is to show **tense**.

Tense tells whether the verb happens in the past, present or future.

← Past	Present ↓	Future →
Simple past tense: ***ed*** is added to words that have already happened (e.g. play → played) Sometimes the word changes completely (e.g. buy → bought).	**Simple present tense:** The verb stays the same or the endings *s* may be added (e.g. play/plays).	**Simple future tense:** *will* is added before the verb (e.g. will play)
was or *were* are added before a verb ending with *ing* (e.g. was playing)	*am, is* or *are* is added before a verb ending with *ing* (e.g. is playing)	*will be* is added before a verb ending with *ing* (e.g. will be playing)

Practice questions

1. Circle two verbs.

   Jenny has the neatest writing in our class. She is also very artistic.

2. Circle the verb group and change it to one verb to make the simple past tense.

   Jenny was helping me with my spelling.

   ____

Day 1

1. Circle the verbs.

   I baked a cake and made some scones.

2. Which tense? past present

   Knowing how to use kitchen appliances is part of cooking.

3. Correct the spelling mistake. ______________

   Do you have cooking lessons at scool?

4. Write the synonym for ***clumsy***. ______________

   steady awkward crooked

5. Add the prefix ***re*** to these words.

   ______appear ______design

6. Write ***cannot*** as a contraction. ______________

7. ***quite*** or ***quiet***?

   I like to cook ______________ a lot of meals at home.

8. What is the singular of ***circuses***? ______________

9. Punctuate the sentence.

   our online grocery order arrives on saturdays

10. Add a comma or commas.

    The order included eggs milk cereal meat and fruit.

11. Add one or more apostrophe to show possession.

    Mums favourite meals are roasts and curries.

12. Circle the nouns.

    I am using a whisk to beat the eggs for the pavlova.

13. Circle the adjective.

    The silver kettle boiled furiously.

14. Change the verb group to one verb to make the simple past tense.

    We <u>were eating</u> all the treats. ______________

15. Insert a full stop and a capital letter to make two sentences.

    We washed the dishes after our meal later we sat down to watch a film together.

Day 2

1. Circle the verb group.
   The confident player is walking onto the field.
2. Change the verb group to one verb to make the simple past tense.
   He is scoring really well. ______________
3. Correct the spelling mistake. ______________
   A libary is a place where books are kept.
4. The underlined word is the antonym for ***finish***.
   Yes ☐ No ☐
   begin final continue
5. Add the suffix ***ation*** to change the verb to a noun.
   prepare ______________
6. Expand the contraction ***didn't***. ______________
7. ***lose*** or ***loose***?
   His tooth became ______________ after a basketball hit him in the mouth.
8. The plural of ***knife*** is ______________.
9. Punctuate the sentence.
   is the basketball final on friday 5 july
10. Is the black comma needed? Yes ☐ No ☐
    Our team's colours are red**,** black and white.
11. Add one or more apostrophes to show possession.
    The teams coach shook hands with the opposing side.
12. Circle the verbs.
    We climbed the stairs into the stands and sat down on the cold seats.
13. Circle the verb group.
    By half-time, the Redbacks were playing far better than the Tigers.
14. Circle two superlative adjectives.
    The Redbacks have the loudest and most enthusiastic supporters.
15. Choose the better word. ***pounced*** ***hopped***
    The Tigers lived up to their name and ______________ like cats on the ball.

Day 3

1. Circle the verbs.
   Make sure that you turn the tap off.
2. Which tense? past present
   Water is our most precious natural resource.
3. Correct the spelling mistake. ______________
   At the begining of winter, we turn on our heating.
4. Is the underlined word a synonym for ***base***?
   Yes ☐ No ☐
   over bottom baseball
5. In the word ***submarine***, the prefix ***sub*** means:
   water under ship
6. Write ***I would*** as a contraction. ______________
7. ***pail*** or ***pale***?
   Another word for a bucket is a ______________.
8. What is the singular of ***stories***? ______________
9. Punctuate the sentence.
   one per cent of water on earth is useable fresh water
10. Add a comma or commas.
    We need water for washing cooking and agriculture.
11. Add one or more apostrophes to show possession.
    About 70 per cent of Earths surface is ocean water.
12. Circle the nouns.
    Gardens can be watered naturally by rain.
13. Circle the adjectives.
    Fresh water is a precious and scarce resource.
14. Change the verb group to one verb to make the simple present tense.
    We will have to conserve water. ______________
15. Insert a full stop and a capital letter to make two sentences.
    Water is needed for us to survive we must use water wisely.

WEEK 3

Day 4

1. Circle the verb group.
   The foul smell of a skunk will stay on its victim for days.
2. Change the verb group to one verb to make the simple past tense.
   The skunk was feeding its young. ______________
3. Write the jumbled word correctly. ______________
   It is ysawla best to avoid a skunk.
4. Circle the antonym for ***smooth***.
   rough   surprised   careful
5. Add ***ly*** to change the adjective to an adverb.
   angry ______________
6. Expand the contraction ***hasn't***. ______________
7. ***could of*** or ***could have***?
   It is likely that a skunk ______________ made a burrow under that woodpile.
8. The plural of ***scissors*** is ______________.
9. Punctuate the sentence.
   do all skunks have black and white markings
10. Add a comma or commas.
    Skunks eat insects fruit worms eggs mice and frogs.
11. Add one or more apostrophes to show possession.
    A skunks spray can travel three metres.
12. Circle the verbs.
    The horned owl is the only animal that attacks skunks for food.
13. Circle two verb groups.
    A skunk will release an odour if it is feeling threatened.
14. Circle the superlative adjective.
    Skunks are some of the bossiest animals.
15. Choose the better word.   ***wisely***   ***foolishly***
    Some animals ______________ avoid the skunk.

Day 5

1. Circle the verbs.
   We saw the sun slowly sink below the horizon.
2. Which tense?   past   present
   We were waiting to see the planets through our telescope.
3. Correct the spelling mistake. ______________
   We are learning about astronomy in sience.
4. Circle the antonym for ***polite***.
   mischievous   rude   pleasant
5. Add ***ly*** to change the adjective to an adverb.
   gentle ______________
6. Expand the contraction ***couldn't***. ______________
7. ***bought*** or ***brought***?
   A child ______________ in their chart of the solar system to display.
8. The plural of ***splash*** is ______________.
9. Punctuate the sentence.
   the planet mercury is the closest to the sun
10. Add a comma or commas.
    Mercury Venus Earth and Mars are the closest planets to the sun.
11. Add one or more apostrophes to show possession.
    The suns gravitation is stronger than a planets.
12. Circle the nouns.
    Astronomers have discovered that many comets enter our galaxy.
13. Circle the adjectives.
    The eager stargazers had been watching the bright comet track across the dark sky.
14. Change the verb group to one verb to make the simple present tense.
    The astronauts were travelling to the moon.
    ____
15. Choose the better word.   ***flew***   ***drove***
    The spacecraft ______________ across the sky and into space.

Skill focus

Adverbs and adverbials

An **adverb** is a word that describes a verb or verb group.

They can change the meaning of the verb by telling how, when, how often and how long it happens for.

This makes the meaning of the verb clearer and more interesting.

(verb) (adverb: how)
My dad **plays** the guitar **beautifully**.

(adverb: when) (verb group)
Lately, he **has been learning** a new song.

(adverb: how often) (verb)
Dad **occasionally brings** his guitar to work to practise.

(verb) (adverb: how long)
Dad **taught** me to play **briefly** before I gave up.

Many adverbs end in ***ly***, but not always.

Sometimes, adverbs may be a group of words that are used to add information to a verb. This is called an **adverbial**. For example:

Adverbial of time (when): The spacecraft was scheduled for lift off **shortly after daybreak**.

Adverbial of time (how): The blast of the engines echoed **long and loud** throughout the valley.

Adverbial of time (where): The astronauts were secured tightly **in their seats**.

Remember, adverbs and adverbials add information to verbs.

Practice questions

1. Add ***ly*** to change the adjectives to adverbs.
   (a) friend ____________
   (b) lazy ____________
2. Circle the adverbs.
   The small children frequently play together. They skipped happily, briefly played ball and eventually rested in the shade.
3. Circle the adverbial of time.
   The children's parents enjoyed watching them play all day long.

Day 1

1. Add ***ly*** to change the adjective to an adverb.
   angry ____________
2. How many adverbs? ____________
   The audience clapped briefly and quickly after each song.
3. Rearrange the letters to make a word that means a type of ***musical instrument***.
   tauigr ____________
4. Write the synonym for ***earlier***. ____________
   yesterday afterwards before
5. In the word ***supermarket***, the prefix ***super*** means:
   star above many
6. Write ***I had*** as a contraction. ____________
7. ***could have*** or ***could of***?
   The concert ____________ been held at a better venue.
8. What is the base word of ***misbehave***?
   Hint: base words have no prefixes or suffixes added.
   ____
9. Write the singular of ***hooves***. ____________
10. Punctuate the sentence.
    is the name of the lead singer jack elton
11. Add one or more apostrophes to show possession.
    The fans ticket was bought at the venues reception.
12. How many verbs? ____________
    Most fans agreed that the concert was a disappointment.
13. Circle the verb group.
    The band was terrible even though they had practised the song many times.
14. Which tense? past present
    The drummer dropped his drumsticks twice.
15. Write the missing verb in its correct form. ***freeze***
    The lead singer ____________ when he forgot the words.

Day 2

1. Add *ly* to change the adjective to an adverb.
   gentle ______________
2. Circle the adverbial of place.
   No one was seriously injured but everyone waited nervously at the scene of the accident.
3. Rearrange the letters to make a word that means a possible cause of ***harm***.
   nerdga ______________
4. Write an antonym for ***continue***. ______________
   begin cease proceed
5. In the word ***anticlockwise***, the prefix ***anti*** means:
   against walk away
6. Expand the contraction ***who'll***. ______________
7. ***quite*** or ***quiet***?
   All was ______________ after the bomb exploded.
8. The base word of ***graceful*** is ______________.
9. Write the plural for ***scarf***. ______________
10. Punctuate the sentence.
    the soldiers name was lieutenant jacobsen
11. Add one or more apostrophes to show possession.
    The soldiers injuries included deep cuts from glass.
12. How many verbs? ______________
    Medics removed glass fragments and cleaned and stitched cuts.
13. Circle the verb group.
    The explosion had shattered windows and damaged tiles on many roofs.
14. Which tense? past present
    One soldier had been knocked unconscious when he hit his head.
15. Write the missing verb in its correct form. ***give***
    Medics ______________ penicillin shots to prevent infection.

Day 3

1. Add *ly* to change the adjective to an adverb.
   happy ______________
2. How many adverbs? ______________
   The hungry polar bears wait patiently for seals to suddenly appear.
3. Correct the spelling mistake. ______________
   It is feared polar bears will become extingt.
4. The underlined word is a synonym for ***accurate***.
   Yes ☐ No ☐
   <u>wrong</u> accepted correct
5. Add the suffix ***ation*** to change the verb to a noun.
   sense ______________
6. Write ***it is*** as a contraction. ______________
7. ***lose*** or ***loose***?
   We had to look carefully so we didn't ______________ sight of the bear's tracks.
8. The base word of ***certainly*** is ______________.
9. Write the singular of ***elves***. ______________
10. Punctuate the sentence.
    do polar bears only live in the arctic
11. Add one or more apostrophes to show possession.
    A polar bears prey is mainly seals.
12. How many verbs? ______________
    When seals come up for air, the polar bear pounces.
13. Circle the verb group.
    Temperatures are rising more quickly in the Arctic than anywhere else in the world.
14. Which tense? past present
    During the winter, polar bears live and hunt for seals on the Arctic sea ice.
15. Write the missing verb in its correct form. ***begin***
    The sea ice is ______________ to melt sooner and takes longer to return.

Day 4

1. Add *ly* to change the adjective to an adverb.

   playful ______________

2. Circle the adverbial of time.

   At the end of the day, Mr Nolan ruthlessly piled on the homework.

3. Write the jumbled word correctly. ______________

   This year, the first day of school is a nedaWesyd.

4. Circle the antonym for ***doubt***. ______________

   believe distrust correct

5. Add ***ally*** to change the adjective to an adverb.

   basic ______________

6. Expand the contraction ***weren't***. ______________

7. ***through*** or ***threw***?

   The ball went ______________ the window.

8. The base word of ***bumpiest*** is ______________.

9. Write the plural of ***calf***. ______________

10. Punctuate the sentence.

    do you know if mrs cadarver still works at the school

11. Add one or more apostrophes to show possession.

    The childs bag was left outside Mr Nolans room.

12. How many verbs? ______________

    Mr Nolan made us do a maths test that took an hour.

13. Circle the verb group.

    Mr Nolan glared at me, as I had been talking to the person next to me.

14. Which tense? past present

    Nothing is worse than the first day of a new school year.

15. Write the missing verb in its correct form. ***forget***

    I had ______________ how to solve the division problems.

Day 5

1. Add *ly* to change the adjective to an adverb.

   awkward ______________

2. How many adverbs? ______________

   Finally, Mum finished ordering her shopping and hastily typed in her credit card details.

3. Correct the spelling mistake. ______________

   The online catelogue listed what was on offer.

4. The underlined word is a synonym for ***exterior***.

   Yes ☐ No ☐

   internal outside exact

5. Add the prefix ***inter*** to these words.

   _____national _____action

6. Write ***it has*** as a contraction. ______________

7. ***bought*** or ***brought***?

   I ______________ several items that were in the sale.

8. The base word of ***instantly*** is ______________.

9. What is the singular of ***leaves***? ______________

10. Punctuate the sentence.

    we ordered a jacket for dads birthday in september

11. Add one or more apostrophes to show possession.

    Mums computer had become slow because of a virus.

12. How many verbs? ______________

    She bought a disk in the computer shop and she installed the anti-virus program.

13. Circle the verb group.

    If the program succeeds, her computer will work faster.

14. Which tense? past present

    Our last online order from this company arrived in three days.

15. Write the missing verb in its correct form. ***hide***

    There were no ______________ costs added to the delivery.

WEEK 4

Skill focus

Types of sentences

A simple sentence is a group of words that form a complete idea.

They are sometimes called an independent clause because they make sense on their own.

All simple sentences have a subject (naming part) and a predicate (telling part).

My best friend is going with me to the cinema.
(subject) (predicate)

Simple sentences can be:

- A **statement**: used to tell something and ends with a full stop.

  I like going to the cinema.

- A **command**: used to give instructions or make requests and ends with a full stop or exclamation mark.

  Ask them what time the film starts.

- A **question**: used to ask something and ends with a question mark.

  What film will we be seeing?

- An **exclamation**: used to express a strong emotion and ends with an exclamation mark.

  I'm so excited to see the film!

Practice questions

1. Underline the subject in red and the predicate in blue.

   The shiny rocket propelled rapidly into the sky.

2. Add punctuation and write the type of sentence: question, command, exclamation or statement.

   (a) Wow, what a take off ☐

   ____

   (b) Go and get the camera ☐

   ____

   (c) What do you think they will see in space ☐

   ____

   (d) Yuri Gagarin was the first man to travel to outer space ☐

   ____

Day 1

1. Circle the subject and underline the predicate.

   The racers approached the finish line.

2. Question ☐, exclamation ☐ or statement ☐?

   Race competitors drive or ride 12 to 14 hours per day ☐

3. Correct the spelling mistake. ____________

   The Dakar Rally is a populer off-road endurance race.

4. In the word ***prehistoric***, the prefix ***pre*** means:

   after   against   before

5. Write ***they had*** as a contraction. ____________

6. Which word comes first in alphabetical order?

   flinch   flight   flimsy   fling

7. ***desert*** or ***dessert***?

   A ____________ is a dry, harsh environment.

8. What is the singular of ***tries***? ____________

9. Punctuate the sentence.

   the dakar rally has been held in south america from 2009 to 2019

10. Circle the verb group.

    Many people have died over the course of the races' history.

11. How many nouns? ____________

    Vehicles in the race include cars, trucks and motorbikes that can travel in sand.

12. Circle the word that does not belong.

    A desert landscape is an ideal similar location for this annual race.

13. How many adjectives? ____________

    The cars travel at blinding speeds and race over terrifying landscapes.

14. The underlined word is a verb. Yes ☐ No ☐

    This thrilling race <u>takes</u> about two weeks to complete.

15. Circle the conjunction.

    Approximately 400 people enter the race, but only two out of five complete it.

Day 2

1. Circle the subject and underline the predicate.
   Mum cooked us a healthy vegetarian meal for dinner.
2. Question ☐, exclamation ☐ or statement ☐?
   Eat good food to stay strong and healthy ☐
3. Rearrange the letters to make a word that is an ***organ of the body***.
   reath ____________
4. Add the suffix ***ment*** to one word to make a new word.
   argue_____ hope_____
5. Expand the contraction ***mightn't***. ____________
6. Which word comes last in alphabetical order?
   spray sprinkle spread sprout
7. ***breath*** or ***breathe***?
   The air we ____________ goes into our lungs.
8. Circle the plural of ***thief***.
   thiefs thieves
9. Punctuate the sentence.
   your heart is slightly bigger than your fist
10. Add a comma.
    Our heart is pear-shaped has four chambers and has valves that open and close.
11. How many nouns? ____________
    Our circulatory system includes the heart, arteries and veins.
12. The underlined word is a: verb adjective
    Our body <u>has</u> several other types of systems.
13. How many adjectives? ____________
    The hard, bony skeleton helps protect the soft internal organs.
14. Circle the noun phrase.
    It also allows us to stand straight and holds up our internal organs.
15. The underlined word is a conjunction.
    Yes ☐ No ☐
    The digestive system takes in nutrients the body needs <u>and</u> gets rid of waste products.

MY SCORE

Day 3

1. Circle the subject and underline the predicate.
   The ancient city of Pompeii was destroyed by a volcanic eruption.
2. Question ☐, exclamation ☐ or statement ☐?
   It's a strange feeling to walk around Pompeii and view the plaster casts of the people who were killed ☐
3. Correct the spelling mistake. ____________
   I would definately like to visit Pompeii in Italy.
4. Add the prefix ***pre*** to these words.
   _____caution _____historic
5. Write ***they will*** as a contraction. ____________
6. Which word comes second in alphabetical order?
   complain compose compare compass
7. ***breath*** or ***breathe***?
   I ran so fast I was short of ____________.
8. What is the singular of ***pyjamas***? ____________
9. Punctuate the sentence.
   volcanic ash mud and rocks covered the cities of pompeii and herculaneum
10. Circle the better word. ***erupting*** ***eruption***
    The volcano's ____________ stopped after 24 hours.
11. How many nouns? ____________
    Many people suffocated when they breathed in ash instead of oxygen from the air.
12. The underlined word is used correctly.
    Yes ☐ No ☐
    A large column of smoke <u>immersed</u> from its centre.
13. How many adjectives? ____________
    Dense, choking ash and molten lava fell like volcanic rain.
14. Circle two adverbs.
    People didn't know whether to shelter safely indoors or flee the city immediately.
15. Circle the conjunction.
    The volcanic ash covered people and preserved details of their bodies.

Day 4

1. Circle the subject and underline the predicate.
   Guide dogs are trained to support people who are blind or have limited vision.
2. Question ☐, exclamation ☐ or statement ☐?
   How long does it take a guide dog to be trained ☐
3. Rearrange the letters to make a word that means ***double forty-five***.
   inteyn ____________
4. Add the suffix ***less*** to one word to make a new word.
   kind_____ pain_____
5. Expand the contraction ***haven't***. ____________
6. Which word comes third in a dictionary?
   strength stretch street streamer
7. ***all ready*** or ***already***?
   Some of the puppies had ____________ commenced guide dog training.
8. The underlined word is the plural of ***city***.
   Yes ☐ No ☐
   citys cities
9. Punctuate the sentence.
   do you know how a dog is chosen and trained to be a guide dog
10. Add commas.
    Qualities needed include intelligence a good memory obedience and calmness.
11. How many nouns? ____________
    A guide dog learns to stop at kerbs, cross the road and go around objects.
12. Circle the collective noun.
    Guide dogs are selected from a litter of pups.
13. Circle two noun phrases.
    You should not pat a guide dog in its working harness.
14. Circle two adverbs.
    Although a guide dog seems to have a hard job, they work happily and tirelessly.
15. Circle the conjunction.
    Food rewards are not given to guide dogs so they won't be distracted.

Day 5

1. Circle the subject and underline the predicate.
   The talented athletes stood proudly for the national anthem.
2. Question ☐, command ☐ or exclamation ☐?
   Listen carefully while the anthem is played ☐
3. Correct the spelling mistake. ____________
   The Olympic Games compitition is held every four years.
4. In the word ***microchip***, the prefix ***micro*** means very:
   large clear small
5. Write ***who is*** as a contraction. ____________
6. Circle the word that comes last in alphabetical order.
   command commence comment common
7. ***breath*** or ***breathe***?
   The sprinter was out of ____________ when she finished the race.
8. The plural of ***watch*** is ____________.
9. Punctuate the sentence.
   the first modern olympic games was held in greece in 1896
10. Circle the verb group.
    The flame of the Olympic Torch is ignited by the sun's rays.
11. Circle the proper nouns.
    In 2012, the Olympic Games was held in London, England.
12. How many collective nouns? ____________
    A crowd of spectators watched the team of athletes warm up.
13. Circle the comparative adjective.
    The talented young equestrian got a higher score than he expected.
14. Circle the adverb.
    His horse easily cleared the fence jumps but not one of the tricky water jumps.
15. Circle the conjunction.
    Despite the humid conditions, most marathon entrants kept running and completed the course.

Skill focus

Pronouns

Pronouns are words that are used in place of a person or thing.

There are many different types of pronouns. They can refer to people, objects and animals.

I	me	you	it	she	her
he	him	us	we	they	them

Some pronouns refer back to the noun or pronoun doing the action in a sentence. These types of pronouns usually end in self (singular) or selves (plural). For example:

John is doing the work **himself**.

They will do the work **themselves**.

Here are other examples of how this type of pronoun is used:

Singular	I	myself
	you	yourself
	it	itself
	he	himself
	she	herself
Plural	you	yourselves
	we	ourselves
	they	themselves

Practice questions

1. Circle the pronouns.

   Gemma and I went to the cinema. We enjoyed ourselves very much.

2. Circle the pronoun and the noun it refers to.

   Gemma usually enjoys spending time by herself after school.

Day 1

1. Circle the pronouns.

   My brother Jack wants me to invite him to my costume party.

2. Circle the pronoun and the noun it refers to.

   Jack has already made his costume all by himself.

3. Write the jumbled word correctly. ______

   I'll email you an itavintino to my birthday.

4. Add the suffix ***ful*** to one word to make a new word.

   mouth______ teeth______

5. Write ***we would*** as a contraction. ______

6. Which word comes second in alphabetical order?

   wreath wreck wrestle wrench

7. ***desert*** or ***dessert***?

   The ______ will be a deliciously rich chocolate cake.

8. What is the singular of ***series***? ______

9. Punctuate the sentence.

   does your party begin at 7 oclock or 8 oclock on saturday

10. Add one or more apostrophes to show possession.

    My partys theme was to come dressed as a character from a well-known TV show or film.

11. Circle the collective nouns.

    My friends brought a bouquet of flowers and several punnets of strawberries.

12. Circle the adverb.

    My costume was excellent, as every guest said I looked exactly like Harry Potter.

13. Circle the conjunction.

    We tried to guess the other characters and who the guest actually was.

14. Circle the adjectives.

    The best costume was made from silky fabric and had square patterns on it.

15. Question ☐, exclamation ☐ or statement ☐?

    We weren't sure at first who came as Iron Man because his mask hid his face ☐

WEEK 6

Day 2

1. Circle the pronouns.

   We have been learning about famous inventors and one day I hope to be like them.

2. Circle the pronoun and the noun it refers to.

   Inventors often find themselves thinking about new ideas.

3. Correct the spelling mistake. ______________

   Telivishon was invented more than 100 years ago.

4. In the word ***autobiography***, the prefix ***auto*** means:

   against self car

5. Expand the contraction ***it'll***. ______________

6. Which word comes second in alphabetical order?

   reflect referee reform refresh

7. ***all ready*** or ***already***?

   The barbecue had ______________ been put together and was to be used.

8. The plural of ***man*** is ______________.

9. Punctuate the sentence.

   alexander graham bell invented the telephone in 1876

10. Add one or more apostrophes to show possession.

    Laszlo Biros invention—the ballpoint pen—became known as the 'biro' in English-speaking countries.

11. Circle the nouns that can't be seen or touched.

    Inventors of machines possess talent and imagination.

12. Circle the adverb.

    Simple machines are cleverly constructed using just a few parts.

13. Circle the conjunction.

    A machine like a tin opener is simple, but others like a computer are complex.

14. Circle the superlative adjective.

    The simple wheel is arguably the most important machine to be invented.

15. Statement ☐, command ☐ or exclamation ☐?

    Take care when using a pair of sharp scissors ☐

MY SCORE

Day 3

1. Circle the pronouns.

   When she was younger, my mum travelled around Europe by herself.

2. Circle the pronoun and its noun.

   Ireland's coastline is very beautiful and it is a great tourist attraction.

3. Rearrange the letters to make a word that means ***to travel***.

   orjuyen ______________

4. Add the suffix ***less*** to one word to make a new word.

   hope______ sad______

5. Write ***who has*** as a contraction. ______________

6. Which word comes third in alphabetical order?

   distress distribute distinct disturb

7. ***wandered*** or ***wondered***?

   We ______________ if there really were leprechauns in Ireland.

8. What is the singular of ***tomatoes***? ______________

9. Punctuate the sentence.

   is the capital city of ireland dublin or cork

10. Add one or more apostrophes to show possession.

    Irelands national flower is the shamrock, which is a clover that has three leaves.

11. Circle the nouns.

    Ireland is called the Emerald Isle because of its green landscape.

12. Circle the adjectives.

    A leprechaun looks like a miniature old man with a green tunic and green hat.

13. Circle the error.

    An amazing Irish fact is that you won't find a wild venomous snake their.

14. The underlined word is a verb. Yes ☐ No ☐

    If you catch a leprechaun, he might lead you to <u>his</u> pot of gold.

15. Question ☐, exclamation ☐ or statement ☐?

    Have you heard about the legend of the Blarney Stone, which is set in the walls of Blarney Castle ☐

MY SCORE

Day 4

1. Circle the pronoun.

   Even though dolphins live in water, they are not fish.

2. Circle the pronoun and the noun it refers to.

   Dolphins rarely live by themselves and usually live together in pods.

3. Correct the spelling mistake. ____________

   A bottlenose dolphin has the abillity to learn tricks.

4. In the word ***megabyte***, the prefix ***mega*** means:

   great   small   middle

5. Expand the contraction ***they'll***. ____________

6. The underlined word comes last in alphabetical order. Yes ☐ No ☐

   ridiculous   <u>riddle</u>   ridge   ridden

7. ***wandered*** or ***wondered***?

   We ____________ around the dolphin enclosure, watching them swim.

8. The plural of ***roof*** is ____________.

9. Punctuate the sentence.

   there is a dolphin that lives in the yangtze river in china

10. Add one or more apostrophes to show possession.

    A dolphins favourite foods are squid, fish and octopus.

11. How many collective nouns? ____________

    From the jetty, a crowd of people could see a pod of dolphins diving through a shoal of fish.

12. Circle the adjectives.

    Dolphins are amazing, as they can be trained to perform complicated and entertaining tricks.

13. Circle the word that does not belong.

    Dolphins take care of each other as they have never been known to help an injured dolphin.

14. The underlined word is a verb. Yes ☐ No ☐

    They <u>communicate</u> with each other using different noises.

15. Question ☐, command ☐ or statement ☐?

    A bottlenose dolphin's curved mouth makes it look as if it's smiling ☐

MY SCORE

Day 5

1. Circle the pronouns.

   Harry's tooth hurt because he had developed a large cavity in it.

2. Circle the pronoun and the noun it refers to.

   The dentist said the cavity would not heal by itself, so Harry would need a filling.

3. Rearrange the letters to make a word that means ***something puzzling***.

   syetmyr ____________

4. Add the suffix ***ous*** to one word to make a new word.

   nature______   poison______

5. Write ***we had*** as a contraction. ____________

6. Which word comes third in alphabetical order?

   display   displease   disrupt   dispose

7. Write ***a*** or ***an***.

   Visiting a dentist doesn't have to be ____________ horrible experience.

8. The singular of ***wives*** is ____________.

9. Punctuate the sentence.

   i have a dental appointment to visit dr buckland on monday

10. Add one or more apostrophes to show possession.

    A tooths hard enamel covering protects its internal parts.

11. Circle the nouns.

    The dentist explained how to care for molars, incisors and gums.

12. Circle the adverb.

    The best thing about frequently visiting the dentist is the fluoride treatment.

13. Is the underlined word used correctly? Yes ☐ No ☐

    Help prevent decay by eating <u>healthily</u> food and drinks.

14. The underlined word is a verb. Yes ☐ No ☐

    Although wisdom teeth are not really needed, most people <u>eventually</u> grow them.

15. Statement ☐, question ☐ or exclamation ☐?

    How often do you visit your dentist ☐

MY SCORE

Skill focus

Prepositions

Prepositions are words that show a connection between nouns and pronouns.

The word ***preposition*** combines the prefix ***pre*** (meaning ***before*** or ***in front of***) and the word ***position***.

So, prepositions are words that are usually 'positioned in front of' nouns and pronouns in sentences.

Prepositions can refer to place, position, time and movement. For example:

Place

He left his shoes **at** the park.

Position

He found them **under** the bench.

Time

He went to the park **after** school.

Movement

He put his shoes **into** his school bag.

There are lots of other prepositions:

about, above, across, around, behind, beneath, beside, between, by, in, inside, near, off, on, out, over, through, to, toward

Can you think of sentences that use these prepositions?

Practice questions

1. Circle the prepositions.

   The curious girl walked through the gate and saw a small rabbit sitting under a tree.

2. Is the underlined word a preposition?

   (a) *The rabbit scurried quickly <u>down</u> its burrow.*
   Yes ☐ No ☐

   (b) *The burrow was <u>hidden</u> carefully under a neat row of bushes.* Yes ☐ No ☐

Day 1

1. Circle the preposition.

   Spectators cheer as contestants run down the hill.

2. The underlined word is a preposition.
   Yes ☐ No ☐

   Contestants and spectators celebrate <u>after</u> the races.

3. Correct the spelling mistake. ______________

   There was an air of exitement at the start of the race.

4. Add a prefix to make the antonym of each word.

   _____agree _____appear

5. ***rowed***, ***road*** or ***rode***?

   The ______________ to the top of the hill was very steep.

6. A synonym for ***combine*** is ______________.

   blend separate collect

7. Number in alphabetical order.

   flash ☐ flask ☐ flare ☐

8. Punctuate the sentence.

   a cheese-rolling competition is held every may in gloucestershire in england

9. Circle who is speaking.

   'Are you entering the race?' asked the official.

10. Add speech marks to show what was said.

    I certainly am! he exclaimed.

11. Circle the verbs.

    Contestants run down a steep hill and they try to catch a wheel of cheese.

12. Which tense? past present future

    The race first began about 200 years ago.

13. Circle the adverbial of place.

    Spectators cheer as contestants run and tumble down the hill.

14. Circle the adverb.

    There are usually several injuries.

15. Write the missing verb in its correct form. ***give***

    The winner is ______________ a fresh wheel of cheese as a prize.

Day 2

1. Circle the preposition.
   Roaming cats do their 'business' in other people's garden beds.
2. The underlined word is a preposition.
   Yes ☐ No ☐
   Cat owners should keep their animals inside their homes.
3. Rearrange the letters to make a word that means ***to find out something***.
   oevdicsr ______________
4. Add the suffix ***ous*** to change the nouns to adjectives.
   humour_____ glamour_____
5. ***he'll, heel*** or ***heal***?
   He said ______________ put a bell around his cat's neck.
6. Is the underlined word an antonym for ***enough***?
   Yes ☐ No ☐
   plenty insufficient extra
7. Number in alphabetical order.
   opponent ☐ opposite ☐ opportunity ☐
8. Punctuate the sentence.
   pet cats can be fluffy cute and friendly
9. Circle who is speaking.
   'Do you leave your cat inside?' my neighbour enquired.
10. Add speech marks to show what was said.
    I replied, We have a dog, not a cat.
11. Circle the verbs.
    Cats climb over walls and fences and get into other gardens.
12. Circle the adjectives.
    Some cats chase helpless birds and make awful noises.
13. Circle the verb group.
    Many birds are killed needlessly by wandering cats.
14. Circle the adverb.
    Dogs can be kept securely in their own garden.
15. Write the missing verb in its correct form. ***find***
    Though some dogs are ______________ to be constantly barking.

MY SCORE

Day 3

1. Circle the preposition.
   There are many species of insect-eating plants around the world.
2. The underlined word is a preposition.
   Yes ☐ No ☐
   Some plants have special hairs that force insects towards their trap.
3. Correct the spelling mistake. ______________
   It is difficult for an insect to excape from a spider's web.
4. Add a prefix to make the antonym of each word.
   _____place _____spell
5. ***flour*** or ***flower***?
   A ______________ is the reproductive part of a plant.
6. A synonym for ***busy*** is:
   active bored lazy
7. Number in alphabetical order.
   antibiotic ☐ antiseptic ☐ anticipate ☐
8. Punctuate the sentence.
   the venus flytrap is a plant that eats bugs flies ants and other insects
9. Circle who is speaking.
   'How do plants catch insects to eat?' asked the girl.
10. Add speech marks to show what was said.
    It has hinged leaves that close like a trap, her dad explained.
11. Circle the verb.
    Nectar attracts insects to the plant.
12. Insert a question word.
    ______________ do digestive juices in the trap dissolve the insect's body?
13. Circle the adverbial of time.
    The sensitive leaves snap shut in less than a second.
14. The underlined word is an adverb. Yes ☐ No ☐
    The trap remains open until an insect lands lightly on its leaves.
15. Write the missing verb in its correct form. ***eat***
    The leaves die after about four meals are ______________.

MY SCORE

WEEK 7

Day 4

1. Circle the prepositions.
   Our homework was written on the whiteboard before school.
2. The underlined word is a preposition.
   Yes ☐ No ☐
   We copied the tasks <u>into</u> our diaries.
3. Correct the spelling mistake. ______________
   An antydote stops the effects of poison.
4. Add the suffix ***ion*** to change the verbs to nouns.
   hesitate_____ inject_____
5. ***rowed***, ***rode*** or ***road***?
   The motor failed so he ______________ the boat to shore.
6. The antonym for ***normal*** is ______________.
   common unusual natural
7. Number in alphabetical order.
   pierce ☐ piece ☐ pier ☐
8. Punctuate the sentence.
   mrs johnson was admitted to the king alfred hospital on tuesday
9. Circle who is speaking.
   'Why was she raced to hospital?' enquired Patrick.
10. Add speech marks to show what was said.
    Mr Patel explained, She had acute appendicitis.
11. Circle the verbs.
    She stayed in hospital over night while she recovered from the surgery.
12. The underlined word is a collective noun.
    Yes ☐ No ☐
    The <u>class</u> expected the maths lesson to be boring.
13. Circle the verb group (three words).
    We will be taught all about multiplication and division for the next two weeks.
14. Circle the adverb.
    The class worked out the answer to each word problem slowly.
15. Write the missing verb in its correct form. ***write***
    We soon got used to ______________ the answers quickly.

MY SCORE

Day 5

1. Circle the prepositions.
   There was a wild storm on Sunday.
2. The underlined word is a preposition.
   Yes ☐ No ☐
   Several tiles on the roof <u>blew</u> into the field.
3. Correct the spelling mistake. ______________
   A ruler will help measure the lengt of this line.
4. Add a prefix to make the antonym of each word.
   _____patient _____possible
5. ***mist*** or ***missed***?
   A ______________ is like a very thick fog.
6. A synonym for ***purchase*** is: ______________
   punish sell buy
7. Number in alphabetical order.
   disturb ☐ distribute ☐ distinct ☐
8. Punctuate the sentence.
   are earths seasons the same on both sides of the world
9. Circle who is speaking.
   'What months have 30 days?' asked Lucy.
10. Add speech marks to show what was said.
    April, June, September and November, replied Bella.
11. Circle the verbs.
    Bella said, 'But February only has 28 days, and 29 in a leap year.'
12. Circle the abstract noun.
    Many people had a lot of anxiety about the upcoming storm.
13. Circle the verb groups.
    It had been raining heavily and we were glad when it stopped.
14. The underlined words are adverbs. Yes ☐ No ☐
    Homeowners had to <u>quickly</u> and <u>tightly</u> secure any loose objects.
15. Write the missing verb in its correct form. ***blow***
    The wind was so strong it ______________ the gate open.

MY SCORE

Day 1

1. Correct the spelling mistake. ______________

   I love to watch a vareyeity of sports.

2. Add the suffix ***ion*** to change the verbs to nouns.

   express______ permit______

3. ***he'll***, ***heel*** or ***heal***?

   I hope the blister on your ______________ will ______________ quickly.

4. The underlined word is an antonym for ***ignore***.
   Yes ☐ No ☐

   observe frighten disregard

5. Number in alphabetical order.

   straight ☐ strange ☐ strength ☐

6. Punctuate the sentence.

   have you watched manchester united play football at their home ground of old trafford

7. Who is speaking? ______________

   'No, but I'd love to!' Tony answered eagerly.

8. Add speech marks to show what was said.

   Would you like to come with me on Saturday? Uncle Patrick asked.

9. Which tense? past present future

   'You know my answer is … yes!' Tony yelled excitedly.

10. Circle the verb group.

    The players were warming up, which is very important.

11. Write the missing verb in the correct form. ***speak***

    Yesterday, the coach ______________ to his team in the changing room.

12. Circle the adverbs.

    Each team ran out energetically onto the ground while the supporters cheered loudly.

13. Circle the pronoun and the noun it refers to.

    The home team celebrated when they scored two goals in quick succession.

14. Circle the prepositions.

    The player dribbled the ball along the ground and kicked it into the net.

15. Insert a question word.

    ______________ did the supporters go to celebrate?

MY SCORE

Day 2

1. Correct the spelling mistake. ______________

   The higher the altitude, the less oxygin in the air.

2. Add the prefix ***pre*** to one word to make a new word.

   drive paid ______________

3. ***rowed***, ***road*** or ***rode***?

   They ______________ on the sledge through the snow on the ______________.

4. The underlined word is a synonym for ***bravery***.
   Yes ☐ No ☐

   cowardice courage brainy

5. Number in alphabetical order.

   decided ☐ deceived ☐ decimal ☐

6. Punctuate the sentence.

   some people dream of climbing mount everest in the himalayan mountains

7. Who is speaking? ______________

   Andre asked, 'Who were the first people to climb it?'

8. Add speech marks to show what was said.

   The mountaineer replied, Edmund Hillary and Tenzing Norgay. It was in 1953.

9. Which tense? past present future

   'I will be one of those successful climbers one day!' Andre exclaimed.

10. Circle the verb group.

    They had travelled cautiously over the icy area.

11. The underlined word is a noun. Yes ☐ No ☐

    Only experienced mountaineers should tackle difficult climbs.

12. Circle the adverbial of time.

    Climbers may have to take shelter for several days in very bad weather.

13. Circle two pronouns.

    Climbers are warned that they should not attempt the climb by themselves.

14. Circle the preposition.

    An avalanche is an event that could occur during a climb.

15. Insert a question word.

    ______________ do avalanches often occur on mountains?

MY SCORE

WEEK 8

Day 3

1. Rearrange the letters to make a word that means ***someone who lives near you***.

   bunoerihg ______________

2. Add the suffix ***ous*** to change the nouns to adjectives.

   fame_____ danger_____

3. ***flour*** or ***flower***?

   She used wholemeal ______________ to make the bread.

4. Circle the antonym for ***calm***.

   nervous normal caring

5. Number in alphabetical order.

   commend ☐ command ☐ comment ☐

6. Punctuate the sentence.

   you should have your ingredients equipment and measuring spoons ready before you start cooking

7. Who is speaking? ______________

   'What are you going to cook for dinner, Harry?' Mum enquired.

8. Add speech marks to show what was said.

   An old favourite—spaghetti bolognese! my brother answered.

9. Which tense? past present future

   'Yum! Everyone likes that!' I replied, licking my lips.

10. Circle the word that is not needed.

    Harry boasted that his special recipe for meatballs with tomato sauce was not the best.

11. Circle the proper noun.

    Harry should wash his hands before cooking.

12. Circle the adverbs.

    Harry quickly made fifteen meatballs and placed them carefully in the sauce.

13. Circle the pronoun and the noun it refers to.

    Harry simmered the meatballs on low heat so they would not break up.

14. The underlined word is a preposition.

    Yes ☐ No ☐

    He drained the cooked spaghetti into the sink.

15. Insert a question word.

    ______________ *can I sprinkle parmesan cheese over them if we don't have any?*

MY SCORE

Day 4

1. Correct the spelling mistake. ______________

   A sunflower has an enormus yellow flower.

2. Add the prefix ***un*** to one word to make a new word.

   teach cooked ______________

3. Write ***to***, ***too*** or ***two*** in the correct places.

   She wanted ______________ pick roses but it was ______________ wet to go outdoors.

4. The underlined word is a synonym for ***entirely***.

   Yes ☐ No ☐

   nothing partly completely

5. Number in alphabetical order.

   relevant ☐ relieve ☐ relation ☐

6. Punctuate the sentence.

   parts of a flowering plant include the seed stem root flower and leaves

7. Who is speaking? ______________

   'What's the name of this conifer?' the lady asked the gardener.

8. Add speech marks to show what was said.

   The gardener replied, It's called a Wollemi pine.

9. Write the missing verb in its correct form. ***find***

   Seeds can be ______________ in a plant's flowers.

10. Circle the word that is not needed.

    If you are cutting rose stems, you should wear a gardening gloves.

11. Circle the nouns.

    Plants grow from seeds and they develop quickly.

12. Circle the adverbial of time.

    A sunflower is fully grown in about three months.

13. Circle two pronouns.

    I grew these sunflowers myself.

14. Circle the prepositions.

    I planted the seedlings beneath the tree which was beside the shed.

15. Circle the collective noun.

    The band of musicians accidentally crushed the plants.

MY SCORE

Day 5

1. Rearrange the letters to make a word that means ***time free from work***.

   lesurie ______________

2. Add the suffix ***ion*** to change the verbs to nouns.

   complete______ locate______

3. ***missed*** or ***mist***?

   The goalkeeper ______________ the ball, which went into the net.

4. Circle the antonym for ***magnify***.

   reduce enlarge magnificent

5. Number in alphabetical order.

   earring ☐ earliest ☐ earth ☐

6. Punctuate the sentence.

   our competition will be on the first friday in august

7. Who is speaking? ______________

   'I've been chosen to compete in the long jump!' my friend Claire told me excitedly.

8. Add speech marks to show what was said.

   That's fantastic! I'm sure you'll do really well! I replied.

9. Write the missing verb in its correct form. ***win***

   Claire easily ______________ the long jump with a record leap.

10. Circle the verb groups.

    I was competing in the high jump and had been waiting for my turn.

11. The underlined word is a noun. Yes ☐ No ☐

    I thought my turn would <u>have</u> come sooner than this.

12. Circle the adverbs.

    I waited patiently for the breeze to stop and I nervously took my turn.

13. Circle the pronoun and the noun it refers to.

    Claire cheered as she watched from the sideline.

14. Circle the prepositions.

    The long-distance runners ran around the track towards the finish line.

15. Circle the proper noun.

    The winner of the javelin competition was from China.

MY SCORE

Skill focus review

1. Correct the spelling mistake. ______________

   It takes eight minites for light from the sun to reach Earth.

2. Add a prefix to make the words mean the opposite.

   ______employed ______natural

3. Write the homophone for ***peace***. ______________

4. Is the underlined word a synonym for ***contented***? Yes ☐ No ☐

   satisfied <u>considered</u> miserable

5. Circle the proper nouns.

   Besides Earth, other planets include Mars, Venus, Jupiter, Saturn and Neptune.

6. Are the underlined words nouns? Yes ☐ No ☐

   The sun is a huge ball of exploding gases and is responsible for our <u>weather</u> and <u>climate</u>.

7. Circle the adjectives.

   The gigantic sun emits powerful rays that are dangerous to humans.

8. Circle the comparative adjective.

   The sun is bigger than Earth.

9. Circle the preposition.

   You could fit 1 300 000 Earths inside the sun!

10. Circle the two pronouns.

    It pulls all other objects in the solar system around itself.

11. Circle the verb.

    Our blue planet is habitable.

12. Which tense? past present future

    Earth's atmosphere protects us from harmful rays.

13. Circle the verb group.

    Earth's atmosphere is comprised of nitrogen, oxygen and other gases.

14. Circle the adverb.

    Many people use sunscreen to effectively protect themselves from the sun's radiation.

15. Question ☐, exclamation ☐ or statement ☐?

    Do you know any facts about the sun ☐

Skill focus

Coordinating conjunctions

A simple sentence expresses a complete idea and has a subject (naming part) and a predicate (telling part).

The old dog is sleeping contently on the couch.
(subject) (predicate)

A simple sentence is sometimes called an **independent clause** because it makes sense on its own.

Often, two simple sentences are joined together using a coordinating conjunction. This forms a **compound sentence**.

Compound sentences help make your writing more interesting.

The most common conjunctions that are used to make a compound sentence can be remembered using the FANBOYS acronym.

F	A	N	B	O	Y	S
for	and	nor	but	or	yet	so

A comma is always used before these conjunctions. For example:

I really like dogs, but they can be very messy!

Practice questions

1. Circle the conjunction in the sentence.
   I had forgotten to finish my homework, so I had to complete it at lunch time.
2. Add a comma before the conjunction.
   I wanted to complete it quickly but it was too long and complicated.
3. Circle the two simple sentences.
   I finished the maths homework first, but I didn't have time to finish the English activity.

Day 1

1. Circle the conjunction.
   Sufficient rainfall is required, or a hot desert will not spring to life.
2. Add a comma before the conjunction.
   The Atacama Desert is smaller than the Sahara Desert yet it is drier.
3. Correct the spelling mistake. ______________
   I love eating both hot and cold chocolate deserts.
4. The underlined word is a synonym for ***intelligent***.
   Yes ☐ No ☐
   dull interesting <u>bright</u>
5. The plural of ***dictionary*** is ______________.
6. Write the homophone for ***meddle***. ______________
7. Expand the contraction ***would've***. ______________
8. Which word comes first in alphabetical order?
   foreign forecast forest
9. Punctuate the sentence.
   the sahara desert in africa is the largest hot desert on earth
10. Are speech marks needed? Yes ☐ No ☐
    The TV show presenter explained that deserts can be hot or cold.
11. Add one or more apostrophes of possession.
    A hot deserts plant life includes shrubs and cacti.
12. Circle the proper nouns.
    The continent of Antarctica which includes the South Pole, is actually a desert as it receives very little rain.
13. Circle the pronoun and the noun it refers to.
    As a huge sandstorm was approaching, the tourists sheltered in a tent to protect themselves.
14. Circle the adverb.
    The sandstorm blew ferociously against the tent.
15. Circle the two noun phrases.
    Their canvas tent was quite effective at keeping out most of the sand.

Day 2

1. The underlined word is a conjunction.
   Yes ☐ No ☐
   Have you ever visited a coral reef, and have you been scuba diving in tropical waters?
2. Circle the two simple sentences.
   Most corals grow in warm, shallow waters, but there are some corals that grow in cold, deep waters.
3. Rearrange the letters to make a word that means ***strange***.
   plcureia ______________
4. An antonym for ***innocent*** is ______________.
   truthful guilty naughty
5. Circle the singular of ***trousers***.
   trouser trousers
6. Write the homophone for ***seen***. ______________
7. Write ***how would*** as a contraction. ______________
8. The underlined word comes second in alphabetical order. Yes ☐ No ☐
   empty emperor emphasis
9. Punctuate the sentence.
   freshwater wetlands are home to trout salmon and catfish as well as birds mammals and insects
10. Are speech marks needed? Yes ☐ No ☐
    Look at that beautiful water lily! she remarked.
11. Add one or more apostrophes of possession.
    The pelicans beak is very large.
12. How many nouns? ______________
    Wetlands include marshes, swamps and bogs and they contain a lot of animals and plants.
13. Circle the pronoun and the noun it refers to.
    The mother bear caught a salmon and devoured it without sharing it with her young cub.
14. Circle the adverb.
    The bear cub looked enviously at its mother as she ate.
15. Circle the prepositions.
    She held the salmon in her claws and sat down to eat it.

MY SCORE

Day 3

WEEK 9

1. Circle the conjunction.
   Mum asked me to sort out the clothes that I'd outgrown, so she could donate them to charity.
2. Add a comma before the conjunction.
   Will my clothes be reused or will they be thrown away?
3. Correct the spelling mistake. ______________
   He had forgoten to wheel out the recycling bin.
4. A synonym for ***fewest*** is ______________.
   most several least
5. The plural of ***tooth*** is ______________.
6. ***past*** or ***passed***?
   The recycling truck drove ______________ our house.
7. Expand the contraction ***hadn't***. ______________
8. Which word comes third in alphabetical order?
   contrary contradict contribute
9. Punctuate the sentence.
   does the recycling truck come once a fortnight on a monday
10. Are speech marks needed? Yes ☐ No ☐
    Dad said to store the extra recycling in the garage.
11. Add apostrophes for possession and contraction.
    The recycling bins lid wouldnt close properly.
12. How many nouns? ______________
    Items made from aluminium, steel, plastic and paper can be recycled.
13. Circle the pronoun and the words it refers to.
    Recycling means collecting old, discarded materials and making new materials from them.
14. Circle the adjectives.
    One way to recycle unwanted clothes that are in good condition is by donating them to a charity shop.
15. Circle the three noun phrases.
    Recycling an aluminium can saves enough energy to run a television set for three hours.

WEEK 9

Day 4

1. The underlined word is a conjunction.
   Yes ☐ No ☐
   The imposing and powerful eagle swooped <u>down</u> quickly, but it missed its wary prey.
2. Circle the two simple sentences.
   The eagle continued its search for food, yet it had no success.
3. Rearrange the letters to make a word that means a ***rural area***.
   cytroun ______________
4. An antonym for ***keep*** is ______________.
   discard remove collect
5. Circle the singular of ***goggles***.
   goggles goggle
6. ***whose*** or ***who's***?
   Do you know ______________ towel this is?
7. Write ***why is*** as a contraction. ______________
8. Which word comes second in alphabetical order?
   screeched scratching scribble
9. Punctuate the sentence.
   the african bush elephant is the largest land animal on earth
10. Are speech marks needed? Yes ☐ No ☐
    What is the fastest land animal? I enquired.
11. Add one or more apostrophes where necessary.
    A cheetahs specialised body creates its amazing speed.
12. Circle the collective nouns.
    We saw a pride of lions and a pack of hyenas.
13. Circle the adverb.
    The young zebra nervously crossed the stream but was stalked by a lion.
14. Circle the adjectives.
    The zebras black and white stripes helped it camouflage in the long, dry grass.
15. Circle two prepositions.
    The zebra went behind the tree and sat under the branches.

MY SCORE

Day 5

1. Circle the conjunction.
   It is easy to make home-made pizza, but you must find a good recipe first.
2. Add a comma before the conjunction.
   Sometimes we feel lazy so we order pizza from the local delivery service.
3. Rearrange the letters to make a word that means ***attractive***.
   utlbaifeu ______________
4. A synonym for ***annoy*** is ______________.
   irritate attack friendly
5. The plural of ***burglar*** is ______________.
6. Write the homophone for ***blew***. ______________
7. Expand the contraction ***couldn't***. ______________
8. The underlined word comes first in alphabetical order. Yes ☐ No ☐
   internal <u>intermission</u> intermediate
9. Punctuate the sentence.
   do you like ham grated cheese pineapple chopped onion and olives on your pizza
10. Are speech marks needed? Yes ☐ No ☐
    Ooh, yes please! I replied, licking my lips.
11. Add one or more apostrophes where necessary.
    Our pizzas bases werent made from wholemeal flour.
12. Circle the abstract noun.
    Having pizza for dinner fills me with happiness.
13. Circle the adverb.
    Our pizzas were so delicious that every slice was quickly gobbled up.
14. Circle the adjectives.
    The hot, gooey cheese burnt our mouths.
15. Circle the two noun phrases.
    On some Saturday nights, we order pizza from a local delivery service.

MY SCORE

Word families

Prefixes and suffixes are often added to base words to create a new word with a different meaning. This can also sometimes change the spelling of the base word.

Words that have the same base word are part of the same **word family**.

A word family is a group of words that are connected in some way.

The word ***respect*** has many other words in its family.

dis**respect**	**respect**ed
respecting	**respect**ful
respectable	**respect**ive
ir**respect**ive	**respect**ably
respectfully	ir**respect**ively

Below are some of the prefixes and suffixes that can be added to ***respect***.

Prefixes	Base words	Suffixes	
dis	respect	ed	able
ir		ing	ly
		ful	ive

Some words often have more than one prefix or suffix added to them to make a new word.

Which words in the ***respect*** family have more than one prefix or suffix added?

Practice questions

1. What are the base words for each of these words?
   (a) stickiness ______________
   (b) glaringly ______________
   (c) respectability ______________
2. Circle two words that can be built from ***explode***.
   explosion explodeful unexploded misexplode

1. The base word of ***successfully*** is ______________.
2. Circle the two words that can be built from ***possible***.
   unpossible impossible possibled possibility
3. Correct the spelling mistake. ______________.
   The continint of Antarctica has no permanent residents.
4. A synonym for ***dull*** is ______________.
   interesting boring daring
5. The singular of ***species*** is ______________.
6. ***Whose*** or ***Who's***?
   ______________ *going to Antarctica with me?*
7. Write ***are not*** as a contraction. ______________
8. Which word comes second in alphabetical order?
   screeched scratching scribble
9. Punctuate the sentence.
   is antarctica surrounded by the southern ocean or the indian ocean
10. Are speech marks needed? Yes ☐ No ☐
    The scientist explained that Antarctica has about 100 research stations scattered across it.
11. Add one or more apostrophes where necessary.
    Antarctica is one of the worlds most important research places as its so untouched.
12. The underlined words are adjectives.
    Yes ☐ No ☐
    Scientists' clothing includes very <u>thick</u> socks, some <u>thermal</u> underwear and a <u>weatherproof</u> jacket.
13. Circle the superlative adjectives.
    Antarctica is unique as it is the coldest, windiest and driest continent of all.
14. Circle the two simple sentences.
    The research team decided to continue in the freezing conditions, but they longed for their warm tents.
15. Question ☐, command ☐ or statement ☐?
    More than 13 000 tourists visit Antarctica each year on commercial ships and private yachts ☐

Day 2

1. The base word of ***uncomfortable*** is ______________.
2. Circle the two words that can be built from ***honest***.
   dehonest honesty dishonest honesting
3. Correct the spelling mistake. ______________
   One of Dad's favorite hobbies is playing golf.
4. A synonym for ***recreation*** is ______________.
   work pleasure build
5. Write the plural of ***quiz***. ______________
6. ***knead*** or ***need***?
   The chef said that you must always ______________ the dough before baking it.
7. ***accept*** or ***except***?
   She ate everything on her plate ______________ the peas.
8. The underlined word comes second in alphabetical order. Yes ☐ No ☐
   <u>either</u> eighteen eighty
9. Punctuate the sentence.
   Dad puts his golf clubs golf bag and golf shoes in his car every saturday morning
10. Are speech marks needed? Yes ☐ No ☐
    Dad said he was picking up his friend, David Booth.
11. Add one or more apostrophes where necessary.
    Dads golf skills arent as good as his friend, Davids.
12. Circle the adverb.
    This is his club and I must return it immediately.
13. Circle the superlative adjective.
    'That's the greatest shot I've ever seen!' exclaimed David. 'Well done!'
14. Circle the conjunction.
    They continued to play golf, and they reached the ninth hole.
15. Exclamation ☐, question ☐ or statement ☐?
    Dad wondered if he'd ever score another hole in one ☐

Day 3

1. The base word of ***undecided*** is ______________.
2. Circle the two words that can be built from ***interest***.
   reinterest interesting uninteresting interestly
3. Rearrange the letters to make a word that means ***to make a picture in your mind***.
   gmiaien ______________
4. An antonym for ***join*** is ______________.
   juggle separate combine
5. The singular of ***libraries*** is ______________.
6. ***passed*** or ***past***?
   In the ______________, there was no roundabout here.
7. Expand the contraction ***mustn't***. ______________
8. Which word comes third in alphabetical order?
   prosperous prospect prosecute
9. Punctuate the sentence.
   road workers installed a roundabout at the busy junction during the month of september
10. Are speech marks needed? Yes ☐ No ☐
    That junction is much safer now, the mayor announced.
11. Add one or more apostrophes where necessary.
    Traffic lights werent an option at the junction.
12. Circle the adjectives.
    Drive carefully around the dangerous bends on the narrow road.
13. Circle the comparative adjective.
    The roundabout certainly proved to be a much safer alternative.
14. Circle the two simple sentences.
    The roundabout was installed, and fewer accidents have occurred at the junction.
15. Exclamation ☐, command ☐ or statement ☐?
    Always obey road rules ☐

Day 4

1. The base word of ***preoccupied*** is ______________.
2. Circle the two words that can be built from ***populate***.
   populated unpopulate repopulate populater
3. Correct the spelling mistake. ______________
   Sertain animals use camouflage to protect themselves.
4. A synonym for ***foolish*** is ______________.
   ridiculous false sensible
5. Write the singular of ***binoculars***. ______________
6. ***knead*** or ***need***?
   Do you know if I ______________ a ticket to get in?
7. ***accept*** or ***except***?
   I ______________ your invitation to the birthday party.
8. Which word comes second in alphabetical order?
   accountant accomplice accompany
9. Punctuate the sentence.
   the zookeeper explained that many animals use camouflage
10. Are speech marks needed? Yes ☐ No ☐
    He told us how chameleons change colour.
11. Add one or more apostrophes where necessary.
    A chameleons eyes pick up colour and signals are sent to the cells in its skin.
12. Circle the adverb.
    A praying mantis skilfully uses its ability to look like a stick.
13. Circle the adjectives.
    Some species of owl have beautiful, white feathers that help it to hide in its snowy habitat.
14. Circle the conjunction.
    A scarlet kingsnake is not poisonous, yet it is coloured like a poisonous coral snake for protection.
15. Exclamation ☐, question ☐ or statement ☐?
    I think a chameleon's ability is amazing ☐

Day 5

1. The base word of ***impossible*** is ______________.
2. Circle the two words that can be built from ***danger***.
   redanger endanger dangerer dangerous
3. Rearrange the letters to make a word that means a ***line without a curve or bend***.
   stgrtiha ______________
4. An antonym for ***willing*** is ______________.
   helpful reluctant wishful
5. Write the singular of ***robberies***. ______________
6. ***passed*** or ***past***?
   John ______________ by the shop on his way to the pool.
7. Write ***how had*** as a contraction. ______________
8. Which word comes third in alphabetical order?
   procession proceeding procedure
9. Punctuate the sentence.
   the cities of beijing in china and new delhi in india are two of the most polluted in the world
10. Are speech marks needed? Yes ☐ No ☐
    What effect has air pollution on people? asked the tourist.
11. Add one or more apostrophes where necessary.
    It can affect peoples health by causing breathing difficulties, sore eyes and sore throats.
12. Circle the adverbs.
    The city's seriously polluted air floated menacingly for miles around.
13. Circle the comparative adjective.
    Humans should exercise greater caution so that dangerous pollutants don't enter the atmosphere.
14. Circle the two simple sentences.
    The pollution must be addressed, or the problems associated with the pollution will increase.
15. Question ☐, command ☐ or statement ☐?
    Waterways can become contaminated when waste is dumped or drained into them ☐

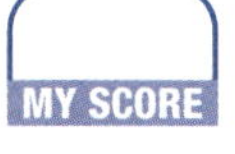

WEEK 10

WEEK 11

Skill focus

Using commas

Commas are useful punctuation.

They help separate words or groups of words in a sentence to help make the meaning clear.

Let's explore two ways that they do this:

Commas after an introduction

A comma is usually placed after a group of words that introduce a sentence.

Often, this happens when a dependent clause is used before the independent clause. For example:

Although dinner will be ready soon, I made myself a sandwich.

Commas for dates and places

Dates

- Use a comma to separate the day from the date, month and year. For example: *Tuesday, 31 May 2022.*

Places

- Use a comma to separate the city and country of a place. For example: *My aunt sent me a postcard from Madrid, Spain.*

Practice questions

1. Punctuate the sentence.

   during the holidays our family went on holiday to Europe.

2. Add a comma.

   We returned home from our holiday on Friday 4 June.

3. Add a comma.

   My favourite place that we visited was Venice Italy.

Day 1

1. Punctuate the sentence.

   one of the most populated cities in the world is Delhi India.

2. Add a comma.

   In 2010 the Commonwealth Games were hosted by Delhi.

3. Correct the spelling mistake. ______________

   India has the second largest populasion in the world.

4. Add a prefix to make the antonym of each word.

   _____rational _____resistible

5. Write the base word for ***bounciest***. ______________

6. The underlined word is a synonym for ***break***.

   Yes ☐ No ☐

   heal fracture drop

7. Write the homophone for ***guest***. ______________

8. The underlined words show what was said.

   Yes ☐ No ☐

   'How many people live in India?' asked the girl.

9. Circle the prepositions.

   Most people have jobs in agriculture, working on farms in the country.

10. Write the missing verb in its correct form. ***find***

    The capital city of Delhi can be ______________ in the north.

11. Circle the verb groups.

    Delhi is believed to be one of the oldest cities in the world, with evidence it was built more than 3000 years ago.

12. Which tense? past present future

    The Australian prime minister will be touring India in July.

13. Circle the adverbial of place.

    The Ganges River flows through one of the most fertile places in the world.

14. Circle the proper noun.

    The Ganges flows through one of the most fertile places in the world.

15. The underlined word is a: pronoun verb noun

    People believe the Ganges is sacred and wash themselves in the river.

MY SCORE

Day 2

1. Punctuate the sentence.
   on friday evening our family went to an indian restaurant for dinner
2. Add a comma or commas.
   We had booked our table for Friday 10 September at five o'clock.
3. Rearrange the letters to make a word that means very pleasing to ***taste***.
   siudloeci ______________
4. Add the suffix ***ous*** to change the nouns to adjectives.
   marvel_____ envy_____
5. Write the base word for ***breathlessness***.
   ____
6. Circle the antonym for ***ordinary***.
   exceptional original average
7. Write the homophone for ***brake***. ______________
8. The underlined words show what was said.
   Yes ☐ No ☐
   '<u>What are the specials on the menu?</u>' enquired my brother.
9. Circle the prepositions.
   We looked over our menus for about five minutes.
10. Write the missing verbs in their correct form. ***choose***
    My brother ___________ butter chicken, but later wished he'd ___________ chicken tandoori.
11. Circle the verb groups.
    As Dad was eating his prawn madras, he noticed the waiter had brought extra rice.
12. Which tense? past present future
    Mum had chosen a very hot dish—beef vindaloo.
13. Circle the adverbs.
    She usually ate chicken but was enjoying this immensely.
14. Circle the abstract noun.
    Mum's face suddenly looked full of worry.
15. The underlined word is a: noun verb pronoun
    'It's so hot I need some water!' <u>she</u> exclaimed as the waiter arrived promptly with a glass.

MY SCORE

Day 3

1. Punctuate the sentence.
   next wednesday i will be celebrating my eleventh birthday.
2. Add a comma or commas.
   I was born on Thursday 19 May 2009 in Darwin.
3. Rearrange the letters to make a word that means ***straight***.
   hzltaroion ______________
4. Add a prefix to make the antonym for each word.
   _____tangle _____selfish
5. Write the base word for ***description***. ______________
6. A synonym for ***believe*** is ______________.
   trust behave doubt
7. Write ***steel*** or ***steal***.
   The construction worker used ______________ in the building.
8. The underlined words show what was said.
   Yes ☐ No ☐
   'Turn that music down!' <u>Mum shouted</u>.
9. Circle the conjunction.
   We didn't think it was loud, but we turned it down anyway.
10. Write the missing verb in its correct form. ***hear***
    'I ______________ it blaring from down the street!' Mum added.
11. Circle the verb groups.
    When you are learning to play an instrument, you will need regular practice.
12. Which tense? past present future
    My sister and I are learning to play the guitar and the drums—it's quite a challenge!
13. Circle the adverbial and its type: time place
    We practised both instruments for about an hour.
14. The underlined words are: adverbs adjectives
    I prefer to play a <u>rhythm</u> guitar than an <u>electric</u> guitar.
15. Add the correct pronoun.
    It's important to clean your guitar strings as you can't play properly when ______________ are dirty.

MY SCORE

WEEK 11

WEEK 11

Day 4

1. Punctuate the sentence.

   while you were sleeping i made your breakfast

2. Add a comma or commas.

   After you have made your bed come and eat your breakfast.

3. Correct the spelling mistake. ______________

   It is sensabel for children to sleep for about 10 hours a night.

4. Add the suffix ***able*** to change the verbs to adjectives.

   solve______   value______

5. Write the base word for ***unreliable***. ______________

6. Circle the antonym for ***whole***.

   entire   fraction   which

7. ***It's*** or ***Its***?

   ______________ *hard to concentrate if you haven't had enough sleep.*

8. The underlined words show what was said.

   Yes ☐   No ☐

   The doctor asked, 'What time do you go to bed?'

9. Circle the conjunction.

   You may be older, yet you don't need as much sleep.

10. Write the missing verb in its correct form. ***sleep***

    When you were a baby, you would have ______________ *for about 16 hours in total each day.*

11. Circle the verb group.

    People have been wondering why we dream when we sleep.

12. Which tense?   past   present   future

    Everybody dreams—but some people don't remember!

13. The underlined words are: adverbs   verbs

    When we are deeply asleep our brain is very active.

14. The underlined word is a: verb   noun   preposition

    Many people dream in colour.

15. Add the correct pronoun.

    My brother talks to ______________ *in his sleep.*

MY SCORE

Day 5

1. Punctuate the sentence.

   when a female turtle has laid her eggs she doesnt look after them.

2. Add a comma or commas.

   Many sea turtle nests can be found on the secluded sandy beaches in Queensland Australia.

3. Correct the spelling mistake. ______________

   Turtles and tortoises are extraordinery reptiles.

4. Add a prefix that means ***to do again***.

   ______fill   ______heat

5. Write the base word of ***irregularly***. ______________

6. A synonym for ***considerate*** is ______________.

   unkind   thoughtful   confident

7. Write the homophone for ***threw***. ______________

8. The underlined words show what was said.

   Yes ☐   ***No*** ☐

   The scientist explained, 'Turtles live most of their life in water, while tortoises live all their life on land.'

9. Circle the prepositions.

   The largest tortoises in the world live on the Galapagos Islands in the Pacific Ocean.

10. Write the missing verb in its correct form. ***swim***

    The turtle ______________ *from one island to another.*

11. Circle the verbs.

    Both creatures lay eggs on land and bury them in sand where they hatch.

12. Which tense?   past   present   future

    The eggs will remain incubating until they hatch.

13. Circle the adverbial and its type.

    duration   place

    Tortoises can live between 70 and 150 years.

14. Circle the nouns.

    A sea turtle uses its flippers to swim in the ocean.

15. Add the correct pronoun.

    Tiny turtles and tortoises, called hatchlings, must look after ______________.

Reported and direct speech

In writing, there are two ways to show what someone has said: **direct speech** and **reported speech**.

Direct speech:

'Do you want a cupcake?' Mum asked.

- The exact words and order are enclosed in speech marks.
- Exclamation marks or question marks are enclosed in the speech marks.
- Usually, a group of words including a verb and the speaker goes at the beginning, middle or end.
- If the speech comes before the speaker, place a comma after the final speech mark; e.g. *'These are nice cupcakes', I told her.*
- If the speech comes after the speaker, place a comma after the speaker and a full stop after the final speech mark; e.g. *I told Mum, 'These are nice cupcakes'.*

Reported speech

Mum asked if I wanted a cupcake.

- This is reported speech.
- The tense and order of the words may change.
- Extra words may also be added, or pronouns might change.
- No speech marks are used.

Practice questions

1. Add a comma and full stop where they are needed.
   (a) *My sister complained 'I want a cupcake too!'*
   (b) *'There is plenty for everyone' Mum reassured her*
2. Circle the sentence type. direct reported
   After we had eaten all the cupcakes, Mum asked us not to tell Dad he had missed out.

Day 1

1. Add a comma and full stop where they are needed.
   'Hello Mrs Magginis' I said, stepping under the ladder to greet her
2. Circle the sentence type. direct reported
   'It's unlucky to walk under ladders!' she exclaimed.
3. Rearrange the letters to make a word that means ***every now and then***.
   alyloacscnoi ______________
4. Add the suffix ***ible*** to change the verbs to adjectives.
   flex______ reverse______
5. The underlined word is the antonym for ***stationary***. Yes ☐ No ☐
   movable motionless <u>standing</u>
6. Write the homophone for ***course***. ______________
7. The singular of ***scales*** is ______________.
8. Punctuate the sentence.
   last saturday a superstitious old lady named mrs magginis moved in next door.
9. Circle the adjectives.
   There are people who think black cats are a sign of good luck.
10. Write the missing verb in its correct form. ***give***
    mrs magginis once ______________ me a fake, stuffed rabbit's foot, which is a good luck charm.
11. Circle the verbs.
    She said bad luck follows those who step on cracks in the pavement.
12. Which tense? past present future
    We watched her avoiding the pavement cracks!
13. The underlined words are: nouns pronouns
    If you knock over a <u>salt</u> shaker, you must toss some salt over your left <u>shoulder</u> to prevent bad luck.
14. Add the correct pronoun.
    A bee in the house means a visitor will arrive, but if you kill ______________, the visitor will not be a welcome guest.
15. Insert a full stop and a capital letter.
    Some people say it's unlucky to open an umbrella inside a house they believe that by doing so, it might start to rain.

MY SCORE

Day 2

1. Add a comma and full stop where they are needed.
   Dad said 'Make sure you wear sunscreen or you will get sunburnt'
2. Circle the sentence type. direct reported
   'What will happen if I get sunburnt?' I enquired.
3. Rearrange the letters to make a word that means a ***long line of people***.
   eeuuq ______________
4. The base word of ***extraordinary*** is ______________.
5. A synonym for ***constantly*** is ______________.
   sometimes considerably always
6. Write ***steel*** or ***steal***.
   The bridge had huge layers of ______________ placed under the concrete.
7. Write the plural of ***echo***. ______________
8. Punctuate the sentence.
   sun protection includes applying sunscreen wearing a hat and wearing sunglasses
9. Circle the prepositions.
   Apply sunscreen over exposed areas of your body throughout the day.
10. Write the missing verb in its correct form. ***burn***
    If you get badly ______________, see a doctor.
11. Circle the verb groups.
    She had realised how much the sun was damaging her skin.
12. Which tense? past present future
    Some people are allergic to particular sunscreens.
13. The underlined words are: adverbs adjectives
    Buying the most <u>expensive</u> sunscreen does not mean it's the <u>most effective</u>.
14. Add the correct pronouns.
    My friend Bob foolishly believes that
    ______________ *can use cooking oil to give*
    ______________ *a tan.*
15. Insert a full stop and a capital letter.
    We wear sunscreen in order to protect our skin however, we should ensure it is waterproof before swimming.

MY SCORE

Day 3

1. Add a comma and full stop where they are needed.
   'Look what happened' said my friend, showing me her plaster-covered arm
2. Circle the sentence type. direct reported
   My friend asked me if I'd ever broken any bones.
3. Correct the spelling mistake. ______________
   There are many fasinating body facts.
4. Add the suffix ***ation*** to change the verbs to nouns.
   multiply______ populate______
5. The underlined word is an antonym for ***certain***.
   Yes ☐ No ☐
   definitely perhaps <u>unsure</u>
6. ***It's*** or ***Its***?
   ______________ *a fact we have 206 bones in our body.*
7. Write the singular of ***hoaxes***. ______________
8. Punctuate the sentence.
   the bones in the body include the patella the skull the ribs the pelvis and the sternum
9. Circle the adjectives.
   I once broke my left wrist when I slipped over and fell on hard ground.
10. Write the missing verb in its correct form. ***have***
    I didn't know I ______________ 52 bones in my feet and ankles.
11. Circle the verb group.
    Our skin is covered in an invisible layer called 'sebum'.
12. Which tense? past present future
    Sebum keeps our skin moist and makes it waterproof.
13. The underlined words are: prepositions conjunctions
    Our 'funny bone' is actually a nerve that extends <u>from</u> the upper arm, <u>across</u> the elbow and <u>down</u> to the hand.
14. Circle the adverbial and its type.
    manner time
    Some people sneeze like an elephant trumpeting!
15. Is the word ***permanent*** used correctly?
    Yes ☐ No ☐
    That permanent injury will be easy to heal.

MY SCORE

Day 4

1. Add a comma and full stop where they are needed.

   The chef announced 'Today I will be showing you how to make a very special dish'

2. Circle the sentence type. direct reported

   The chef explained how to make sushi wrapped in seaweed.

3. Correct the spelling mistake. ____________

   My favourite ice cream flavour is chokolat.

4. The base word of ***glaringly*** is ____________.

5. A synonym for ***foe*** is ____________.

   friend family enemy

6. Write another homophone for ***pear/pare***.

   ____

7. Write the plural of ***atlas***. ____________

8. Punctuate the sentence.

   red algae is collected as food in places like finland japan and iceland

9. Circle the prepositions.

   Seaweed is wrapped around the fillings inside sushi.

10. Write the missing verb in its correct form. ***be***

    In Scotland, sheep liver, lungs and heart ____________ mixed with oats, placed inside a sheep's stomach and boiled for an hour.

11. Circle the verb groups.

    Gazpacho soup is made from finely chopped, raw vegetables and is served cold.

12. Which tense? past present future

    I will try frog's legs and snails one day.

13. The underlined word is a: pronoun verb

    Snails are removed from their shell and cleaned before they are put back.

14. Add the correct pronoun.

    If you taste a frog's leg, you'll probably agree ____________ tastes like chicken.

15. Is the word ***postponed*** used correctly?

    Yes ☐ No ☐

    The dinner party was postponed until further notice.

MY SCORE

Day 5

1. Add a comma and full stop where they are needed.

   'Today our class will be watching a video about the aye-aye' my friend announced

2. Circle the sentence type. direct reported

   'The aye-aye was first thought to be a rodent!' the scientist on the video exclaimed.

3. Rearrange the letters to make a word that means the opposite of ***cheap***.

   psevxiene ____________

4. Add the suffix ***ation*** to change the verbs to nouns.

   inform______ vaccinate______

5. The underlined word is an antonym for ***enough***.

   Yes ☐ ***No*** ☐

   plenty empty insufficient

6. Write another homophone for ***seize/seas***.

   ____

7. Circle the singular for ***volcanoes***. volcano volcanoe

8. Punctuate the sentence.

   Found only in Madagascar the aye-aye is an unusual mammal

9. Circle the adjectives.

   Aye-ayes have an unusual appearance—large yellow eyes, enormous ears and a bushy tail.

10. Write the missing verb in its correct form. ***be***

    The most peculiar feature ____________ its hands.

11. Circle the verb groups.

    Its long middle finger is used to tap on branches and can find hollows where insects hide.

12. Which tense? past present future

    The aye-aye scoops out an insect with its long finger.

13. The underlined word is an: adverb adjective

    Many Malagasy are terribly frightened by its spooky facial appearance and witch-like hands.

14. Circle the adverbial and its type.

    manner duration

    An aye-aye's incisor teeth grow throughout its life.

15. Is the word ***temporary*** used correctly?

    Yes ☐ No ☐

    Aye-ayes in zoos live in this temporary home forever.

MY SCORE

WEEK 12

WEEK 13

Skill focus

Subordinating conjunctions

An **independent clause** expresses a complete idea and has a subject (naming part) and a predicate (telling part). For example:

The boy sang happily.

A **dependent clause** is a group of words that also have a subject and a predicate, but do not make sense on their own. For example:

As he walked home from school.

A dependent clause must be joined with an independent clause to make sense. This is done using conjunctions such as:

after	although	as	because	before
if	since	until	when	while

This makes a **complex sentence**.

Conjunctions can be placed between two clauses:

*The boy sang happily **as** he walked home from school.*

They can also start a sentence:

***As** the boy walked home from school, he sang happily.*

When the dependent clause is used at the start of a sentence, a comma is placed after it.

Practice questions

1. Is a comma needed?

   (a) *Since it is my birthday I asked Mum if we could have take-away tonight.*
   Yes ☐ No ☐

   (b) *Mum said that I could choose dinner because my brother was allowed to on his birthday.*
   Yes ☐ No ☐

2. Circle the conjunction.

   While we ate our dinner, Mum prepared the birthday cake.

Day 1

1. Is a comma needed? Yes ☐ No ☐

   Although they were skilled explorers the tourists had been lost for many days.

2. Circle the conjunction.

   They desperately needed to be rescued soon if they were going to survive.

3. Correct the spelling mistake. ______________

   I thought that was an exelent film, do you agree?

4. A synonym for ***afraid*** is ______________.

   courageous foolish frightened caring

5. Add a prefix to make the words mean the opposite.

   _____honest _____order

6. The contraction ***he's*** can mean ______________ or ______________.

7. Write the homophone for ***steal***. ______________

8. Write the plural of ***baby***. ______________

9. Punctuate the sentence.

   since it is so hot and dry very little vegetation grows in desert landscapes

10. Add speech marks to show what was said.

    We flew over the Sahara Desert! Luke explained.

11. Circle the abstract noun.

    When they eventually found water, they were filled with relief.

12. Circle the proper nouns.

    The group had been lost in the Gobi Desert since Monday; their hope of being found diminished with each hour that passed.

13. The underlined words are:

    verb groups collective nouns

    The people desperately hoped they would not encounter a <u>plague of locusts</u> or a <u>pride of lions</u>.

14. Circle the adjectives.

    The conditions were hot and dry.

15. Circle the preposition.

    A rescue plane circled above.

Day 2

1. Is a comma needed? Yes ☐ No ☐

   I have been playing netball since I was five years old.

2. Circle the conjunction.

   My netball skills are improving because I rarely miss a goal.

3. Correct the spelling mistake. ______________

   It is important to comunikate with your teammates.

4. The underlined word is the synonym ☐ or antonym ☐ for ***courage***.

   amazement   <u>cowardice</u>   excitement

5. Add the suffix ***ment*** to change the verbs to nouns.

   fulfil______   govern______   enjoy______

6. The contraction ***I'd*** can mean ______________ or ______________.

7. Write the homophone for ***serial***. ______________

8. Write the plural of ***half***. ______________

9. Punctuate the sentence.

   will your team be competing in the netball finals on sunday 22 september

10. Circle the sentence type. direct   reported

    The coach told us to pack our skirt, collared shirt, bib and sports socks.

11. Circle the nouns.

    Many balls went whizzing by as we spectated from the crowded grandstand.

12. Circle the proper nouns.

    Rita Egan and Una Jones scored the most goals for their teams.

13. Circle two pronouns.

    The girls were handed gold trophies, and they held them up proudly.

14. Circle two adjectives.

    The team played an exciting match and the enormous crowd loved it.

15. Circle the preposition.

    The players stood on the stage and gratefully accepted their championship medals.

Day 3

WEEK 13

1. Is a comma needed? Yes ☐ No ☐

   Africa is a very interesting continent to learn about because it has many unique animals and beautiful landscapes.

2. Circle the conjunction.

   Although most of Africa has a hot climate, some of its mountains are capped with snow.

3. Correct the spelling mistake. ______________

   My neece is working as a volunteer in Africa.

4. A synonym for ***hide*** is ______________.

   expose   conceal   remove

5. Add a prefix to make the words mean ***half***.

   ______circle   ______detached

6. The contraction ***that's*** can mean ______________ or ______________.

7. Write the homophone for ***aloud***. ______________

8. Write the plural of ***hero***. ______________

9. Punctuate the sentence.

   while you were on holiday which african countries did you visit

10. Add speech marks to show what was said.

    I have been to Morocco, Tanzania and Kenya, replied Hugh.

11. Circle the proper nouns.

    Amy is visiting Madagascar on her holiday; she hasn't been abroad before.

12. Circle the adverbs.

    Amy carefully gathered her things and packed them neatly into her suitcase.

13. The underlined words are:

    verb groups   collective nouns

    Amy <u>had seen</u> lions and zebra when she was in Botswana.

14. ***its*** or ***it's***?

    When ______________ hot, the animals gather at the waterholes to drink.

15. Circle the word that is not needed.

    When she returned back home, Amy had many photos to show her friends.

Day 4

1. Is a comma needed? Yes ☐ No ☐

   We did not start the film until everyone was ready.

2. Circle the conjunction.

   When everyone was comfortable, I pressed play.

3. Unjumble the jumbled word. ______________

   Many different ganlseuag are spoken throughout the world.

4. The antonym for ***permanent*** is ______________.

   heritage   temporary   antique

5. Add the suffix ***ous*** and change the nouns to adjectives.

   danger______   poison______

6. The contraction ***you'd*** can mean ______________

   or ______________.

7. Write the homophone for ***bear***. ______________

8. Write the singular of ***pupils***. ______________

9. Punctuate the sentence.

   Dad boasted come and see this amazing cake ive just made!

10. Circle the sentence type.   direct   reported

    'I made rocky road with chocolate marshmallows peanuts and coconut', I told him.

11. Which verb best expresses the meaning—***stalked***, ***walked*** or ***ran***?

    The thief ______________ *around the house silently.*

12. Circle the adverb.

    The audience watched the screen intently.

13. Circle two pronouns.

    The brilliant actors had outdone themselves; they had performed better than ever before.

14. Circle two adjectives.

    The action-packed film was entertaining.

15. Circle the preposition.

    The actor in the play gave a brilliant performance.

MY SCORE

Day 5

1. Is a comma needed? Yes ☐ No ☐

   While my parents were waiting in the queue to vote I quietly read my book.

2. Circle the conjunction.

   I couldn't vote as I'm not 18.

3. Correct the spelling mistake. ______________

   If you must intarupt, sir, please do so politely.

4. The underlined word is the synonym ☐ or antonym ☐ for ***hostile***.

   friendly   <u>aggressive</u>   cordial   insincere

5. Add a prefix to make the words mean the opposite.

   ______regular   ______responsible

6. The contraction ***she's*** can mean ______________

   or ______________.

7. Write the homophone for ***herd***. ______________

8. Write the plural of ***country***. ______________

9. Punctuate the sentence.

   the lengthy debate became very heated between the two politicians

10. Add speech marks to show what was said.
    Hint: speech marks only go around the words that are said.

    Order! the speaker shouted. I said order!

11. Circle three nouns.

    Voters had been waiting for the announcement for many hours.

12. Circle the proper nouns.

    Helen Smithers was named Prime Minister of New Zealand for another term.

13. The underlined words are:

    verb groups   collective nouns

    The Australian leader kindly greeted the visiting <u>party of politicans</u>.

14. Is the word ***dejected*** used correctly?
    Yes ☐ No ☐

    Members of the opposition looked dejected when they heard the results.

15. Circle the prepositions.

    Flags were raised along the street and I saw them blowing in the breeze.

MY SCORE

Skill focus

Where do words come from?

Did you know that the word:

- **aquarium** comes from the Latin word *aqua*, meaning ***water*** and *arium*, meaning ***a place***?

- **geography** comes from the Greek word *geo*, meaning ***earth*** and *graphos*, meaning ***to write about***?

Many of the words we use originally come from other languages. These are known as **root words**.

Root words are often used as prefixes or suffixes.

They do not usually make sense on their own.

Knowing where words come from, and their meaning, can help us work out the meaning of some unknown words.

To work out the meaning of a root word, think about how other words that share the same root word are similar.

Practice questions

Match the root words to their meanings.

between   two   half

1. The root ***bi*** as in ***bicycle*** and ***biplane*** means ____________.
2. The root ***inter*** as in ***interact*** and ***interview*** means ____________.
3. The root ***semi*** as in ***semicircle*** and ***semifinal*** means ____________.

Day 1

WEEK 14

1. The root ***cycl*** as in ***cyclone*** and ***bicycle*** means:
   triangular   rectangular   circular
2. Write the word part that means ***earth***. ____________
   geologist
3. Correct the spelling mistake. ____________
   The weather in Greece was bewtiful.
4. The antonym for ***artificial*** is ____________.
   articulate   authentic   phony
5. Expand the contraction in context. ____________
   *Hint: **'s** can mean **is** or **has**.*
   I think he's going to be late; he usually is.
6. Add the suffix ***ness*** to change the adjectives to nouns.
   like______   fair______   bold______
7. Write the homophone for ***mare***. ____________
8. Punctuate the sentence.
   would you like some lemons from our tree hannah asked
9. Add apostrophes to show possession.
   A plums juice stained Pauls hand.
10. The black comma is correct.   Yes ☐   No ☐
    *I chopped apples, pears, bananas**,** and oranges for the fruit salad.*
11. Circle the collective noun.
    We bought a punnet of strawberries.
12. Circle the two verbs.
    The hen scavenged and scratched around the vegetable garden.
13. Circle the adjective.
    People should eat five servings of vegetables per day.
14. Add ***juicy*** in the superlative form.
    This orange is the ____________ I have ever eaten.
15. Circle the conjunction.
    Before we could pick the fruit, it had fallen off the tree.

WEEK 14

Day 2

1. The root ***photo*** in ***photograph*** and ***photocopier*** means:

   light   water   earth

2. Write the word part that means ***circular***. ____________

   cyclical

3. Unjumble the jumbled word. ____________

   Do you prefer sunny trehwae or thunderstorms?

4. Write ***accept*** and ***except*** in the correct places.

   I can't ____________ your invitation as I'm working every day ____________ Sunday this week.

5. Which word comes first after ***excite*** in alphabetical order?

   excrete   excess   excuse   excursion

6. Circle two words that can be built from ***system***.

   systemming   systematic   antisystem   ecosystem

7. Write the singular of ***men***. ____________

8. Punctuate the sentence.

   kieran enquired What's the weather like outside

9. Add apostrophes to show contraction.

   As its warm, Helens wearing a skirt and Jodys wearing shorts.

10. Add speech marks to show what was said.

    Whales can sometimes be seen along the South African coastline, my sister informed me, reading aloud from her book.

11. The underlined word is a:

    collective noun   proper noun.

    I saw a pod of whales from the cliff this afternoon.

12. Circle the two verbs.

    A cow and her calf swam side by side, their flippers rising occasionally.

13. Circle the two pronouns.

    I wanted them to come back again tomorrow.

14. Circle the proper noun.

    The ocean around South Africa is filled with marine life.

15. Circle the conjunction.

    We didn't get back to the cliff top for a week because of the heavy rains.

MY SCORE

Day 3

1. The root ***port*** in ***portable*** and ***transport*** means:

   important   carry   self

2. Write the word part that means ***carry***. ____________

   export

3. Correct the spelling mistake. ____________

   You must study hard if you want to acheeve good results.

4. The underlined word is a synonym ☐ or antonym ☐ for ***glorious***?

   magical   magnificent   horrible

5. Expand the contraction in context.
   *Hint: **'d** can mean **had** or **would**.*

   ____

   I'd like to study to be a doctor when I finish school.

6. Add a prefix to make the words mean the opposite.

   ____possible   ____probable

7. Write the homophone for ***waist***. ____________

8. Punctuate the sentences.

   dad is a barber and mum is a nurse id like to be a lawyer when i grow up

9. Add an apostrophe to show possession.

   The boys pencil scratched quietly on his page.

10. Add speech marks to show what was said.

    How did your test go today, love? Mum enquired.

11. Write the missing verb in its correct form. ***write***

    Have you ____________ the instructions down?

12. Rewrite in the simple past tense.

    I am reading my book. ____________

13. Write the missing pronoun.

    ____________ *studied for their tests together.*

14. Add ***hard*** in the comparative form.

    Jane studied ____________ than the other children.

15. Circle the conjunction.

    Please put down your pencils as your test is now finished.

Day 4

1. The root ***peri*** in ***perimeter*** and ***periscope*** means:

   around earth measure

2. Write the word part that means ***light***. ____________

   photon

3. Rearrange the letters to make a word that means ***not curved***.

   tsiarthg ____________

4. ***dessert*** or ***desert***?

   The delectable ____________ tasted delicious.

5. The underlined word comes first in alphabetical order. Yes ☐ No ☐

   urgent urban <u>urchin</u> Uranus

6. What is the base word of ***unknowingly*** and ***acknowledge***?

   ____

7. Write the singular of ***echoes***. ____________

8. Punctuate the sentence.

   are you going to help me make the cake she asked.

9. Add apostrophes to show contraction.

   'Whats your favourite dessert?' asked Mum.

10. Add a comma.

    Flour banana and sugar are four important ingredients in this recipe.

11. Write the missing verb in its correct form. ***grease***

    Have you ____________ this tray?

12. Rewrite in the simple past tense.

    We were eating the desserts we made.

    ____

13. Circle the comparative adjective.

    My family decided Mum's dessert was tastier than mine.

14. Circle the proper noun.

    Chef Michel has won many awards for his desserts and is world famous.

15. Circle the conjunction.

    Desserts are great but should only be eaten in moderation!

MY SCORE

Day 5

1. The root ***cent*** in ***century*** and ***percentage*** means:

   ten hundred thousand

2. Write the word part that means ***water***. ____________

   aquatic

3. Rearrange the letters to make a word that means to ***recall*** or ***relive***.

   mebremre ____________

4. The antonym for ***damage*** is ____________.

   destroy repair devastate rearrange

5. Expand the contraction in context. ____________

   I'd already seen the film, so we chose another one.

6. Add the suffix ***less*** and change the nouns to adjectives.

   hope______ care______ talent______

7. Write the homophone for ***plain***. ____________

8. Punctuate the sentence.

   Since the water is so clean there must be fish in that lake

9. Add an apostrophe to show possession.

   That turtles tank has many plants and rocks in it.

10. Add commas.

    In addition to the fish you can find turtles frogs tadpoles and eels in that lake.

11. Write the missing verb in its correct form. ***try***

    We couldn't catch any frogs, even though we ____________ hard.

12. Rewrite in the simple past tense.

    They were catching frogs.

    ____

13. Circle the adjectives.

    Those slippery, slimy frogs have escaped from our nets.

14. Add ***slimy*** in the superlative form.

    The ____________ fish slid quickly through my hands.

15. Circle the conjunction.

    Because of the recent rainfall, the lake will be teeming with fish and frogs soon.

Skill focus

Using apostrophes

Apostrophes are a type of punctuation that can be used to show possession.

Using apostrophes this way can sometimes be confusing.

Here are some hints to help you avoid common mistakes.

Where does the apostrophe go?

The apostrophe to show ownership goes straight after the owner or owners.

The tail of the apostrophe always points to the owner or owners.

Example: *the boy's mother, the ladies' golf clubs, the men's bags*

Do I always need to add s?

When a word ends in ***s*** (usually a plural noun), we usually only add an apostrophe, not another ***s***.

Example: *the dogs' tails, the ladies' handbags*

Are apostrophes used to show a plural?

Apostrophes are never used to make plural nouns.

✓ *My favourite TV shows are on tonight!*

✗ ~~*My favourite TV show's are on tonight!*~~

Practice questions

For each sentence, add an apostrophe to show possession.

(a) *Several childrens bags had been left scattered across the footpath.*

(b) *The childrens faces didn't look happy when they had arrived at their classrooms.*

(c) *Two helpful children quickly picked up all of their classmates bags.*

Day 1

1. Add an apostrophe to show possession.
   Those peoples dogs are playing happily together.
2. Circle the correct phrase.
   the puppie's balls *the puppies' balls*
3. Correct the spelling mistake. ______________
   My mum is turning fourty this September.
4. A synonym for ***gather*** is ______________.
   steal collect scatter prevent
5. The root ***geo*** in ***geography*** and ***geology*** means:
   water earth great
6. Expand the contraction in context. ______________
   I am not sure that's going to fit in the cupboard.
7. Write the homophone for ***peace***. ______________
8. Punctuate the sentence.
   do you want to come to my birthday party on friday 9 july maxine asked
9. Add speech marks to show what was said.
   Happy birthday Hannah! her friends exclaimed.
10. The black apostrophe shows possession ☐ or contraction ☐.
    Unfortunately, I won't be going to Maxine's party.
11. Circle the common noun.
    Which kind of cake do you prefer: Devil's Food or Black Forest?
12. Are the underlined words adjectives ☐ or adverbs ☐?
    'What a <u>rich</u> and <u>decadent</u> cake', she commented loudly and excitedly.
13. Circle the pronoun.
    The guests hoped that he would enjoy his birthday gifts.
14. Circle the preposition.
    The carefully wrapped gifts lay on the table.
15. Circle the conjunction.
    Celebrating birthdays is fun, although I wish my birthday was in the summer.

Day 2

1. Add an apostrophe to show possession.

   The ladies dresses were elaborately decorated.

2. Circle the correct phrase.

   the lady's sunglasses *the ladys' sunglasses*

3. Correct the spelling mistake. ______________

   The spy was very good at disguising his identitee.

4. The underlined word is a synonym ☐ or an antonym ☐ for ***defend***.

   protect <u>attack</u> destroy guard

5. Add a prefix to make the words mean the opposite.

   _____usual _____common

6. Expand the contraction in context. ______________

   The rubbish that's been sitting there for a week smells terrible, please take it out to the bin.

7. Write the homophone for ***past***. ______________

8. Punctuate the sentence.

   is she departing for her latest mission on sunday 7 november

9. Add a comma to the list.

   The agency purchased new surveillance equipment recording devices and a camouflaged vehicle.

10. Does this word need an apostrophe?

    Yes ☐ No ☐

    These <u>gadgets</u> are developed using the latest technology and high-tech materials.

11. Circle the common nouns.

    The camera was operated by Miss Maxwell, who was hiding in the cupboard.

12. Circle the adverbs.

    She hid silently until the group finally left the room.

13. Circle the pronouns.

    She quickly gathered her belongings and packed them into her bag.

14. Circle the preposition.

    Miss Maxwell got into the van.

15. Circle the conjunction.

    Her boss would be angry if she arrived late to their meeting.

MY SCORE

Day 3

1. Add an apostrophe to show possession.

   The musicians instruments were on the stage.

2. Circle the correct phrase.

   two drummers' drumsticks

   two drummer's drumsticks

3. Correct the spelling mistake. ______________

   There was a lot of rain last night and water was dripping from our ceeling in the hallway.

4. The synonym for ***confess*** is ______________.

   lie admit speak

5. The root ***tri*** in ***tripod*** and ***triangle*** means:

   ten three two

6. Expand the contraction in context. ______________

   Check on the internet to see what's on at the cinema.

7. Write the homophone for ***guest***. ______________

8. Punctuate the sentence.

   have you heard the weather forecast for tomorrow james asked politely

9. Add speech marks to show what was said.

   The wild weather has damaged many properties, the reporter explained.

10. Add two apostrophes to show contraction.

    Its been raining a lot more than it normally would this time of year, dont you agree?

11. Who is speaking? ______________

    'Tom and Ger, don't forget your umbrellas', Mum called out.

12. Write the missing verb in its correct form. ***watch***

    Were you ______________ the lightning last night during the storm?

13. ***its*** or ***it's***?

    Did the dog spend the night in ______________ kennel to stay out of the rain?

14. Question ☐, command ☐ or statement ☐?

    You must evacuate before the storm hits ☐

15. Is the word ***postponed*** used correctly?

    Yes ☐ No ☐

    Due to the weather, the event has been postponed.

MY SCORE

WEEK 15

Day 4

1. Add one or more apostrophes to show possession.
   The umpires whistles created a racket at the tennis courts.
2. Circle the correct phrase.
   childrens' coaches   children's coaches
3. Rearrange the letters to make a word that means very strange or odd. ***dweir***
   ____
4. The antonym for ***complex*** is ____________.
   difficult   simple   immense   continuous
5. Add the suffix ***ant*** to change the verbs to adjectives.
   observe_____   tolerate_____
6. Expand the contraction in context. ____________
   'What's been going on in here?' Dad yelled.
7. Write the homophone for ***whose***. ____________.
8. Punctuate the sentence.
   what would you do if you found a large sum of money asked Daniel
9. Add commas.
   He found an old damaged leather wallet that was heavy with cards cash receipts and coins.
10. Add apostrophes to show possession.
    Daniels honesty was recognised when the wallets owner, Mr Hassan, offered him a reward for returning it.
11. Who is speaking? ____________.
    'Daniel, thank you kindly for returning my wallet', said Mr Hassan.
12. Write the missing verb in its correct form. ***spend***
    Daniel ____________ *some of the money Mr Hassan had given him.*
13. Write ***award*** or ***reward***.
    Daniel added the rest of the ____________ *money to his savings.*
14. Question ☐, command ☐ or statement ☐?
    Where did you find my wallet ☐
15. Is the word ***expanded*** used properly?
    Yes ☐   No ☐
    'I didn't expect he'd give me a reward', Daniel expanded to his envious friends.

MY SCORE

Day 5

1. Add one or more apostrophes to show possession.
   Our bodys blood vessels carry food and oxygen to our cells.
2. Circle the correct phrase.
   a person's skeleton   *a persons' skeleton*
3. Correct the spelling mistake. ____________
   Dad and I went to the kemist to collect our medicine.
4. The underlined word is a synonym ☐ or antonym ☐ for ***decay***?
   freeze   rot   fall   boil
5. The root ***aqua*** in ***aquarium*** and ***aquaplane*** means:
   fire   wind   water
6. Expand the contraction in context. ____________
   What do you think he's done wrong now?
7. Write the homophone for ***two*** and ***to***. ____________
8. Punctuate the sentence.
   a special guest is coming to our school on wednesday 10 march
9. Add speech marks.
   Who is the special guest? the children enquired.
10. The black apostrophe shows possession ☐ or contraction ☐?
    Mrs Smith's class weren't sure who to expect.
11. Who is speaking? ____________
    'I am pleased to introduce the talented chemical scientist, Mrs Brown!' announced Mrs Smith to her class.
12. Write the missing verb in its correct form. ***bring***
    Mrs Brown ____________ *some children to the front to help her with the exciting experiments.*
13. ***its*** or ***it's***?
    'Children, please remember that ____________ *dangerous to perform these experiments at home', warned Mrs Brown.*
14. Circle the preposition.
    During one experiment, Mrs Brown showed us how to make a balloon float above our heads.
15. Circle the conjunction.
    After the show, we made a card to thank Mrs Brown for coming to our school.

MY SCORE

Day 1

1. Rearrange the letters to make a word that means to ***be gone all of a sudden***.

   pareadsip ____________

2. Circle the plural of ***valley***.

   vallies valleys

3. Add a prefix to make the words mean the opposite.

   _____connect _____respect

4. ***drawer*** or ***draw***?

   Lisa had to clean out her messy ____________ at school.

5. Number the words in alphabetical order.

   merit ____ meringue ____ mermaid ____

6. Circle the two words that can be built from ***appear***.

   reappear appearance deappear appearly

7. Punctuate the sentence.

   have you ever seen a magician perform live

8. Add a comma.

   Many years ago I saw a magician perform in France.

9. Add an apostrophe to show possession.

   The magicians show was impressive but maybe just a little too long.

10. Circle the adverb.

    His main trick was amazingly done; he escaped from chains while submerged in water.

11. Circle the pronouns.

    He stayed under the water for almost five minutes! It was intense to witness!

12. Circle the noun.

    When did the show finish?

13. Circle the superlative adjective.

    We all agreed, it was the most amazing show we had ever seen.

14. Circle the conjunction.

    Although it was late by the time we left the arena, everyone was full of energy.

15. The underlined word is a preposition ☐ or a noun ☐?

    Rigged <u>above</u> the stage, the lighting added a lot to the show.

MY SCORE

Day 2

1. Correct the spelling mistake. ____________

   The captain had to make a choyce; either turn back to the harbour or try to weather the storm.

2. Write the plural of ***echo***. ____________

3. The root ***quad*** in ***quadrangle*** and ***quadruplets*** means:

   four leg three

4. Write the homophone for ***weight***. ____________

5. Expand the contraction in context. ____________

   Do you think you'd ever go skydiving?

6. The synonym for ***dense*** is ____________.

   thin thick soft runny

7. Punctuate the sentence.

   ships which become wrecked often turn into popular dive sites

8. Circle the sentence type. direct reported

   The dive master instructed us to prepare all our equipment.

9. Add an apostrophe to show possession.

   The fishs fins were brightly coloured.

10. Circle the abstract noun.

    My bravery surprised me when I saw a small shark.

11. Circle the verb group.

    The divers had stayed under for too long; their oxygen barely lasted.

12. Circle the pronoun.

    The boat's captain seemed upset with himself when the boat hit a turtle.

13. Circle the adjectives.

    There are many popular diving sites along the coastline.

14. Circle the conjunction.

    The divers were tired, yet all agreed it had been a fantastic day.

15. Circle the preposition.

    We looked across to see land.

WEEK 16

WEEK 16

Day 3

1. Correct the spelling mistake. ____________

   If you make a mistake erase it and rewrite the correct arnser.

2. Write the plural of ***family***. ____________

3. Add a suffix meaning ***without***.

   blame_____ child_____ use_____

4. Write the homophone for ***threw***. ____________

5. Expand the contraction in context. ____________

   I think you'd better clean your room now, while you can still see the floor!

6. What is the base word of ***leadership*** and ***mislead***?

   ____

7. Punctuate the sentence.

   its dangerous to ride your bike without a helmet

8. Add commas.

   The professional skater's board was black orange purple and yellow.

9. The black apostrophe is for possession ☐ or contraction ☐?

   The bike's handlebars were custom made for the rider, who'd spent a lot of money.

10. The underlined word is a collective noun ☐ or a common noun ☐?

    The <u>crowd</u> watched as the skater skated.

11. Circle the three pronouns.

    They were surprised when the skater removed her helmet; she was a girl!

12. Circle the nouns.

    She took her skateboard and helmet and sat down on the bench for a rest.

13. Add ***talented*** in the comparative form.

    I'm a ____________________ *skater than he is.*

14. Circle the conjunction.

    Do you prefer to ride your bike or your scooter?

15. Circle the preposition.

    He sped down the track quickly.

Day 4

1. Correct the spelling mistake. ____________

   There was a breef meeting between the two politicians last Wednesday.

2. Write the singular of ***cherries***. ____________

3. The word ***fossil*** comes from the Latin word ***fossilis*** meaning:

   clean up dig up

4. Write the homophone for ***wait***. ____________

5. Expand the contraction in context. ____________

   When he's tired he becomes very grumpy and irritable.

6. The antonym for ***daring*** is ____________.

   bold boring cautious

7. Punctuate the sentence.

   how many hours of sleep do you usually get each night

8. Circle the sentence type. direct reported

   'I have told you for the last time Gillian Black—bed!' Dad growled.

9. Add an apostrophe to show possession.

   The childrens bedtime is at 8 p.m.

10. Circle the adverb.

    I usually sleep for a good eight and a half hours.

11. Circle the verb group.

    My friend has slept over at my house before.

12. Write the missing pronoun.

    We set up the tent in the back garden all by ____________.

13. Circle the adjectives.

    We laid comfortably on the soft grass and looked up at the bright stars.

14. Circle the conjunction.

    When the weather is cold, I like to go to bed early.

15. Circle the preposition.

    The children got into bed quietly.

Day 5

1. Rearrange the letters to make a word that comes after seventh and before ninth.

   ithghe ______________

2. Write the singular of ***pianos***. ______________

3. Add a prefix to make the words mean the opposite.

   _____selfish _____healthy

4. Write ***aisle*** and ***Isle*** in the correct places.

   I sat in the ______________ seat on the ferry trip over to the ______________ of Skye.

5. Which word comes before ***remind*** in the dictionary?

   reminisce remiss remember

6. Circle two words that can be built from ***music***.

   non-musical unmusic musician musication

7. Punctuate the sentence.

   many children in the school have caught the chickenpox virus

8. Add a comma.

   Before they turn one babies are usually given multiple vaccinations.

9. Add apostrophes to show possession.

   Are the babys vaccinations up to date?

10. The underlined noun is collective ☐ or proper ☐?

    The <u>team</u> of medical experts worked to find a cure for the illness.

11. Circle the pronoun and the noun it refers to.

    Doctor Smith said he had seen this particular disease before.

12. Circle the nouns.

    Parents should give their children vaccinations as these will protect them from contracting diseases.

13. Circle the superlative adjective.

    Alexander Fleming's most important discovery was penicillin, now used to treat many diseases and illnesses.

14. Circle the conjunction.

    Before Jim was diagnosed, he had visited many different doctors.

15. The underlined word is a preposition ☐ or a noun ☐?

    <u>Over</u> the last decade, there have been many medical advances made.

Skill focus review

WEEK 16

1. Correct the spelling mistake. ______________

   A cactus is a particuler kind of plant that can grow well in hot desert regions.

2. Add a prefix to make the antonym of each word.

   _____place _____spell

3. ***rowed***, ***road*** or ***rode***?

   He ______________ through the desert to see the cactus plants.

4. Which word comes second in alphabetical order?

   scribble scratching screeched

5. The base word of ***explosion*** is ______________.

6. What part of the word means small in ***microscope*** and ***microbiology***?

   ____

7. Add one or more apostrophes to show possession.

   Mexicos deserts have more than 500 species of cactus.

8. The underlined phrase is correct. Yes ☐ No ☐

   the cactus' leaves <u>the cactus's leaves</u>

9. Add speech marks.

   Do cactus plants live only in desert areas? queried the girl.

10. Circle the sentence type. direct reported

    The botanist told the girl that cactus grow in desert or semi-desert areas.

11. Add a comma.

    A rare cactus with a beautiful white flower is found only in Brazil South America.

12. Add a comma before the conjunction.

    Cactus plants are beautiful but beware of their sharp thorns.

13. Circle the conjunction.

    The stems of an aloe vera cactus are filled with a soothing gel, and it is often used to treat burns.

14. Circle the conjunction.

    Although cacti live in dry climates, they have many adaptations that help them survive.

15. Is a comma needed? Yes ☐ No ☐

    Since a cactus needs water its long roots spread deep into the soil.

MY SCORE

WEEK 17

Skill focus

Similes

A simile is a figure of speech that compares one thing with another using the words ***as*** or ***like***. For example:

My aunt is ***as blind as a bat****.*

The friends were ***like two peas in a pod****.*

My baby sister is ***as sweet as honey****.*

That boy climbs ***like a monkey****.*

Comparing what two things have in common makes writing more interesting.

It helps to create a picture in the reader's mind.

Practice questions

1. Complete the similes.
   (a) *As quiet as a ______________.*
   mouse   zebra
   (b) *Work like a ______________.*
   horse   cat
2. Circle the simile.
   With a smile as sweet as sugar, the little girl thanked her mum for her new doll.

Day 1

1. Complete the simile. ***leaf*** or ***bone***?
   As dry as a ______________.
2. Circle the simile.
   The girl ran as quick as lightning to get away from the barking dog.
3. Rearrange the letters to make a word that means ***happens very often***.
   tylfrqeune ______________
4. The underlined word is a synonym ☐ or antonym ☐ for ***gorgeous***.
   beautiful   unattractive   enormous
5. Add the suffix ***ness*** to change the adjectives to nouns.
   sick______   dark______   kind______
6. The contraction ***she's*** can mean ______________ or ______________.
7. Write the homophone for ***groan***. ______________
8. Write the singular of ***knives***. ______________
9. Punctuate the sentence.
   the forgetful farmer didnt close the gate so some cows got out onto the road
10. Add commas.
    Cows sheep pigs ducks and chickens are all raised on that farm.
11. Add two apostrophes to show possession.
    The ducks egg was much bigger than the chickens.
12. Underline the adjectives.
    The old farmhouse needed a new roof.
13. Rewrite in the simple present tense.
    They fed the cows. ______________________
14. Write ***its*** or ***it's***.
    The clumsy old cow injured ______________ leg when it became caught in the fence.
15. Which verb better expresses the meaning—***hurried*** or ***strolled***?
    He ______________ along the path casually.

Day 2

1. Complete the simile. ***rock*** or ***bear***?

   As solid as a ______________.

2. Circle the simile.

   I didn't like what Mum cooked, so I ate my dinner as slow as a snail.

3. Correct the spelling mistake. ______________

   We ate at a very nice restaurant where the food was really dilicous.

4. An antonym for ***identical*** is ______________.

   alike different similar genuine

5. Add a prefix to make the words mean ***do before***.

   _____paid _____school

6. The contraction ***it's*** can mean ______________ or ______________.

7. Write the homophone for ***mussel***. ______________

8. Write the plural of ***lady***. ______________

9. Punctuate the sentence.

   william shakespeares plays have been performed around the world for 400 years

10. Add speech marks to show what was said.

    She cried out from the audience, No! Don't do it!

11. Add apostrophes for contraction and possession.

    Women werent allowed to act in Shakespeares time, so all womens parts were played by men.

12. How many nouns? ______________

    Shakespeare's popular play 'Hamlet' is one of his most famous.

13. The underlined words are verb groups ☐ or prepositions ☐?

    The dedicated actors <u>had been rehearsing</u> for many hours and <u>were becoming tired</u>.

14. Circle the adverb.

    The audience watched the play intently.

15. Circle the conjunction.

    Watching a play at an outdoor theatre is a great experience, unless it rains!

Day 3

1. Complete the simile. ***rake*** or ***pancake***?

   As flat as a ______________.

2. Circle the simile.

   Dad was as busy as a bee doing work around the house.

3. Correct the spelling mistake. ______________

   A powerfull eagle soared effortlessly through the sky.

4. The underlined word is the synonym ☐ or antonym ☐ for ***honest***.

   pleasant insincere <u>truthful</u>

5. Add the suffix ***ible*** to change the verbs to adjectives.

   force_____ access_____ reverse_____

6. The contraction ***it'd*** can mean ______________ or ______________.

7. Write the homophone for ***stationary***.

   ____

8. Write the plural of ***nanny***. ______________

9. Punctuate the sentence.

   have you ever seen an eagle swoop to catch its prey

10. Add commas to the list.

    An eagle's diet can include small mammals fish other smaller birds and lizards.

11. Add an apostrophe or apostrophes to show possession.

    A large eagles wingspan can extend over two metres.

12. Circle the adverb.

    Stealthily, the eagle swooped towards its prey.

13. The underlined words are: verb groups/ noun phrases

    <u>The unsuspecting rabbit</u> was grabbed by the eagle.

14. Circle the pronoun and the noun it refers to.

    The eagles cared for the eaglets and fed them each morning.

15. Circle the conjunction.

    Eaglets stay with their parents until they are about 11 weeks old.

MY SCORE

WEEK 17

WEEK 17

Day 4

1. Complete the simile. ***tin*** or ***nails***?

   As hard as ______________.

2. Circle the simile.

   Mum was as brave as a lion while she was removing that spider from the house.

3. Correct the spelling mistake. ______________

   The preshious ring was worth a lot of money.

4. The antonym for ***ordinary*** is ______________.

   unusual boring friendly

5. Add a prefix to make the words mean ***do again***.

   _____make _____arrange

6. The contraction ***they'd*** can mean ______________ or ______________.

7. Write the homophone for ***prints***. ______________

8. Write the plural of ***arch***. ______________

9. Punctuate the sentence.

   did the womans engagement ring have diamonds and rubies in it

10. Add speech marks to show what was said.

    The woman screamed out, Help, my jewellery has been stolen!

11. Add an apostrophe for contraction or possession.

    The burglars fingerprints were left on the window.

12. Write the missing verb in its correct form. ***steal***

    Many people have had their jewellery ______________.

13. Rewrite in the simple future tense (two verbs).

    Somebody stole it. ______________________

14. ***loose*** or ***lose***?

    Are you absolutely certain you didn't just ______________ it somewhere?

15. Is the word ***targeting*** used correctly?

    Yes ☐ No ☐

    The thieves had been targeting homes when people were away on holidays.

Day 5

1. Complete the simile. ***ice*** or ***water***?

   As cold as ______________.

2. Circle the simile.

   Harry was as proud as a peacock when he won the race.

3. Rearrange the letters to make a word that means a ***place where ships dock***.

   brhuora ______________

4. An antonym for ***precious*** is ______________.

   cheap valuable expensive

5. Add the suffix ***ly*** and change the adjectives to adverbs.

   honest_____ foolish_____ smooth_____

6. The contraction ***why's*** can mean ______________ or ______________.

7. Write the homophone for ***witch***. ______________

8. Write the singular of ***dwarves***. ______________

9. Punctuate the sentence.

   the harbour in hong kong is one of the busiest in the world

10. Add commas to the list.

    Ships import and export livestock grains manufactured goods and textiles.

11. Add apostrophes for possession and contraction.

    Didnt the ships captain see the other boat?

12. Write the better verb. ***parked*** ***docked***

    The massive ship ______________ in the harbour at midnight.

13. Rewrite in the simple future tense.

    We watched the ships come in.

    ____

14. ***sight*** or ***site***?

    The harbour is a popular tourist ______________.

15. Which verb—***praised*** or ***refused***?

    The captain ______________ the crew for their efforts.

Skill focus

More comma uses

Commas are used to separate words or groups of words in a sentence. They help make the meaning clear.

Let's explore two ways they do this.

Commas for additional information

A pair of commas can be used in the middle of a sentence to separate words that provide the reader with extra information.

My birthday cake, covered with fresh cream and berries, was delicious.

One comma is placed at the beginning of the extra information and the other is placed at the end.

If this extra information is taken out, the sentence still makes sense.

My birthday cake, covered with fresh cream and berries, was delicious.

Commas to clarify meaning

Let's eat Dad

Let's eat, Dad.

Using a comma helps make the meaning of your writing clear.

Without a comma, this sentence has a completely different meaning.

Practice questions

1. Add a comma to clarify meaning.

   While the chicken was roasting Mum and I chopped the vegetables.

2. Add a comma to enclose the extra information.

   The dinner we made which had taken two hours to prepare was delicious.

Day 1

WEEK 18

1. Add a comma to clarify meaning.

   While we were eating the reporter on television warned us about the natural disaster.

2. Add commas to enclose the extra information.

   Tsunamis caused by an underwater earthquake often cause catastrophic damage.

3. Correct the spelling mistake. ____________

   Surfing lessons were a popyuler activity at the camp.

4. Add a prefix to make the words mean ***do wrong***.

   ____spell ____treat ____use

5. Write ***wary*** and ***weary*** in the correct places.

   The tired and ____________ surfers were ____________ of sharks in the water.

6. Expand the contraction in context. ____________

   It'd been a really long time since I had seen him.

7. Circle two words that can be built from ***claim***.

   exclaim unclaim reclaimed claimness

8. The underlined word is the synonym ☐ or antonym ☐ for ***polite***?

   friendly rude courteous meek

9. Punctuate the sentence.

   the 2004 boxing day tsunami devastated many asian countries

10. Add apostrophe(s) to show contraction.

    There wasnt much warning of the tsunami before its arrival.

11. The underlined words are common nouns ☐ or proper nouns ☐?

    The presidents and leaders of many countries offered assistance to the affected areas.

12. Circle the conjunction.

    Since the tsunami, people have worked to rebuild their lives and communities.

13. Circle the adverbial of duration.

    People continued to search for their missing relatives for many months.

14. Circle the collective noun.

    Many teams of volunteers helped the local people.

15. Circle the simile.

    The wall of water created by a tsumami is as tall as a mountain.

WEEK 18

Day 2

1. Add a comma to clarify meaning.

   If you can send us a postcard from the mountains.

2. Add commas to enclose the extra information.

   The mountain which loomed over the town was finally covered in snow.

3. Rearrange the letters to make a word that means ***bad*** or ***unpleasant***.

   lfawu ____________

4. Which root word means ***very small***?

   mega   micro   auto

5. ***alter*** or ***altar***?

   Can I please ____________ my booking?

6. Which word comes directly before ***fudge*** in alphabetical order?

   fruit   fuel   fulfil   frost

7. What is the base word of ***unreported*** and ***reportedly***? ____________

8. The underlined word is the plural of ***fly***.
   Yes ☐   No ☐

   flys   flies

9. ***break*** or ***brake***?

   I really enjoyed the ski trip, though unfortunately I did ____________ my arm in a bad fall.

10. Are speech marks needed?   Yes ☐   No ☐

    Mark said that Japan is the most interesting country he has visited.

11. Circle the nouns.

    We packed jackets, scarves and gloves for our ski holiday.

12. Circle the abstract noun.

    He showed amazing courage on the slopes.

13. Circle the conjunction.

    Mum prefers to go to the beach but we all like the snow the best.

14. Circle the pronouns.

    If I could go back there tomorrow I would, it was such a great holiday!

15. Complete the simile.   ***cloud***   ***rock***

    The snow was as soft as a ____________.

MY SCORE

Day 3

1. Add a comma to clarify meaning.

   I like cooking cats and going to concerts.

2. Add commas to enclose the extra information.

   The concert which had sold out months ago was the best I had ever seen.

3. Correct the spelling mistake. ____________

   The children all had a wunderfull time at the circus.

4. Add the suffix ***en*** to change the adjectives to verbs.

   soft______   length______   sharp______

5. Write the homophone for ***night***. ____________

6. Expand the contraction in context. ____________

   It's been raining all week! When will it ever stop?

7. Circle three words that can be built from ***go***.

   ongoing   goed   went   ungoing   undergo

8. The antonym for ***achieve*** is ____________.

   try   fail   do   go

9. Punctuate the sentence.

   think about the greatest concert youve ever seen, our music tutor instructed

10. Add apostrophe(s) to show possession.

    Henrys guitar lessons were paying off as he was improving each day.

11. Underline the object noun phrase.

    The energetic lead singer accidentally broke his guitar.

12. Write ***for*** or ***in***.

    Everyone in my family has a passion ____________ music and can play with great talent.

13. How many verbs? ____________

    Music is great in so many ways; it can improve your mood, motivate you and entertain you.

14. Add a preposition.   ***in***   ***across***

    Friends of ours are lucky to have a studio ____________ their house.

15. Circle the simile.

    The music was as loud as thunder.

Day 4

1. Add a comma to clarify meaning.

   I am bringing Jane John and Jack are going together.

2. Add commas to enclose the extra information.

   The actress who has red hair played her role well.

3. Correct the spelling mistake. ____________

   The label must be attashed if you return the dress.

4. Which root word means ***earth***?

   geo photo cent

5. Write the homophone for ***meet***. ____________

6. The underlined word comes first in alphabetical order. Yes ☐ No ☐

   money <u>Monday</u> monarch moment

7. What is the base word of ***moisturise*** and ***moisten***?

   ____

8. Write the singular of ***beaches***. ____________

9. ***their*** or ***they're***?

   Do you know if ____________ coming?

10. Are speech marks needed? Yes ☐ No ☐

    Marcie asked if I wanted to see the new film with her.

11. Write the missing words.

    The actress took off ____________ sunglasses and signed autographs for ____________ fans, who were very grateful.

12. Write the missing verb in its correct form. ***take***

    Stars are constantly having their picture ____________ by paparazzi and fans.

13. Rewrite in the simple future tense.

    He went to LA. ____________________

14. Circle the pronouns.

    He made a name for himself in Hollywood.

15. Complete the simile. ***bird*** ***flower***

    The actress was as pretty as a ____________.

MY SCORE

Day 5

1. Add two commas to clarify meaning.

   Mum washes Dad and I dry and my sister packs away the dishes.

2. Add commas to enclose the extra information.

   My parents who met at school have lots of fun together.

3. Correct the spelling mistake. ____________

   'What a deliteful bunch of flowers!' she exclaimed.

4. Add a prefix to make the words mean the opposite.

   ______correct ______active

5. Write the homophone for ***would***. ____________

6. Expand the contraction in context. ____________

   They'd like to travel to Japan for their next holiday.

7. Circle three words that can be built from ***satisfy***.

   dissatisfied satisfaction satisfiedly unsatisfied

8. The underlined word is a synonym ☐ or antonym ☐ for ***victory***?

   triumph <u>defeat</u> success

9. Punctuate the sentence.

   do you think that all family members should help with the housework

10. Add apostrophes for possession and contraction.

    In our house, Dad doesnt work and Mum does, so Dads job is to look after us and keep the house tidy.

11. Write the missing pronoun.

    Women used to be the only ones who would have stayed home in the past. All of the housework was done by ____________.

12. ***Whose*** or ***Who's***?

    '____________ left their socks lying around again?' Dad demanded.

13. Circle the pronoun and the noun(s) it refers to.

    Mum and Dad make a good team—they work well together.

14. Rewrite in the simple future tense.

    I cleaned my room. ____________________

15. Circle the simile.

    My mum and dad are like two peas in a pod.

MY SCORE

WEEK 18

Skill focus

Modal verbs

Verb groups are verbs that have two parts—one or more helping verbs and a main verb. For example:

*I wonder what we **are having** for dinner.*

(helping verb) (main verb)

In some verb groups, the helping verb changes the meaning of the main verb. They make the verb stronger or weaker.

Some of these helping verbs are:

must	will	would	should	can	could	may	might
Strength of verb							
strongest ←							→ weakest

They can tell how likely something is to happen:

*We **might be having** pizza for dinner.*

They can give advice or show an obligation to do something:

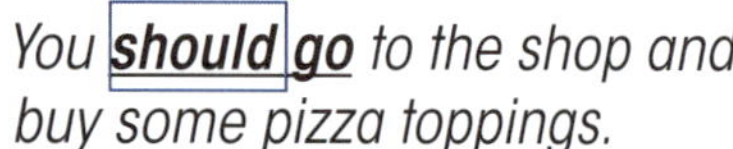

*You **should go** to the shop and buy some pizza toppings.*

They can also show the ability to perform the verb:

*I **can make** the pizza dough while we wait.*

Practice questions

1. Circle three verb groups.

   Mum said I must catch the bus at four o'clock, so I should go, or I might be late.

2. Add the helping verb that shows a stronger obligation. ***must*** ***should***

   I ____________ run quickly because Mum will be worried if I am late.

Day 1

1. Circle the verb group.

   You must travel by train if the ferry makes you seasick.

2. Add the verb that shows ability. ***can*** ***might***

   If you think the train takes too long, you ____________ fly instead.

3. Rearrange the letters to make a word that means a ***place to wash clothes***.

   rydualn ____________

4. The antonym for ***freeze*** is ____________.

   chill thaw cool crack

5. Add the suffix ***able*** and change the verbs to adjectives.

   avoid______ cure______ enjoy______

6. Expand the contraction in context. ____________

   'Why's the sky blue?' the boy asked innocently.

7. Write the homophone for ***through***. ____________

8. Write the singular of ***messes***. ____________

9. Punctuate the sentence.

   how many ways are there to travel across the english Channel

10. Add commas.

    You can travel by ferry train or even fly in an aeroplane! Cars buses and motorbikes can also be taken across on the ferries.

11. Add an apostrophe to show possession.

    Standing on the Cliffs of Dover, you can see Frances coastline across the channel.

12. Circle the proper noun.

    The Channel Tunnel was officially opened in 1994.

13. Write the comparative or superlative form for ***fast***.

    The train is ____________ than the ferry.

14. Circle the preposition.

    We bought the train tickets on the internet.

15. Circle the conjunction.

    People can travel by ferry, train or aeroplane while cars, buses and motorbikes can be taken across on the ferries.

Day 2

1. Circle the verb group.

   You should volunteer to clean up your local area.

2. Add the helping verb that shows a weaker obligation. ***must*** ***could***

   You ______________ organise a community event to encourage others to care for their community.

3. Correct the spelling mistake. ______________

   It is important for people to look after the inviroment.

4. A synonym for ***accurate*** is ______________.

   nasty correct wrong different

5. Add a prefix to make the words mean the opposite.

   _____equal _____expected

6. Expand the contraction in context. ______________

   What's being done to help save water in your area?

7. Write the homophone for ***peace***. ______________

8. ***shore*** or ***sure***?

   A lot of rubbish and waste washed up on the ______________ after the ship sank.

9. Punctuate the sentence.

   plastic bags are often eaten by sea creatures who think the bags are jellyfish

10. Circle the sentence type. direct reported

    The class asked what they could do to help.

11. The black apostrophe shows possession ☐ or contraction ☐?

    The world's oceans are becoming more polluted as too many people don't care about the problem.

12. Circle the simile.

    The community works together to make the local area as clean as a whistle.

13. Circle the adjectives.

    Yesterday, Martin found an expensive watch in the thorny bushes.

14. How many pronouns? ______________

    The watch belonged to a poor man. It was given to him by his grandfather.

15. Circle the conjunction.

    Before the watch was returned, the man had been quite upset.

MY SCORE

Day 3

1. Circle the verb group.

   We might be going on a camping holiday this year.

2. Add the helping verb that shows a stronger obligation. ***must*** ***could***

   We ______________ pack a torch so we can see in the dark.

3. Correct the spelling mistake. ______________

   My grandmother takes a lot of medicashion.

4. The underlined word is a synonym ☐ or antonym ☐ for ***prevent***?

   help <u>permit</u> stop choose

5. Add the suffix ***ful*** to these nouns.

   youth_____ colour_____ success_____

6. Expand the contraction in context. ______________

   When's Dad going to be home, Mum?

7. Write the homophone of ***knew***. ______________

8. Write the plural of ***monkey***. ______________

9. Punctuate the sentence.

   how long until we have a break the tired climber enquired

10. Add a comma to the list.

    The heavy packs contained tents sleeping bags and food supplies.

11. Add one or more apostrophes.

    The group hadnt been asleep long when they heard a womans shout in the distance.

12. Circle the abstract noun.

    The shaken woman told the other campers about the events that had given her a fright.

13. Is the word ***described*** used correctly?

    Yes ☐ No ☐

    The woman, who had left her tent to go to the toilet, described a creature with yellow eyes.

14. Circle the pronoun and the noun it refers to.

    The guide explained, 'That is just an owl. It has eyes that look scary in the dark!'

15. Circle the conjunction.

    Although the woman felt a little bit silly, the others were glad to hear the creature was harmless.

MY SCORE

WEEK 19

Day 4

1. Circle the verb group.

   Thomas can play football really well.

2. Add the helping verb that shows a stronger possibility. ***will*** ***may***

   He ____________ be the striker at our match this weekend.

3. Correct the spelling mistake. ____________

   Unfortunately, the star player injured her sholder before the volleyball final.

4. The synonym for ***weary*** is ____________.

   trustworthy tired suspicious

5. Add a prefix to make the words mean the opposite.

   ____afraid ____known

6. Expand the contraction in context. ____________

   The coach told us she's got to have an X-ray.

7. Write the homophone for ***sail***. ____________

8. ***your*** or ***you're***?

   Where will you display ____________ trophy?

9. Punctuate the sentence.

   do you think we can win without kim one of the players asked

10. Circle the sentence type. direct reported

    The coach replied, Of course you can, you're a fantastic team!

11. Add an apostrophe.

    What time is the big match next week, or dont you know yet?

12. Circle the simile.

    Mum and Dad were as excited as puppies as they watched the match from the sidelines.

13. Insert the better adjective. ***related*** ***injured***

    The ____________ player, who had to miss the match, cheered the team on.

14. Circle the preposition.

    Surprisingly, the opposing team from Canberra lost the match.

15. Circle the conjunction.

    Winning a grand final is a great experience, so I hope we win again next year, too!

MY SCORE

Day 5

1. Circle the verb group.

   You must follow the road rules.

2. Add the helping verb that shows a weaker possibility. ***will*** ***may***

   If you do not follow the rules, you ____________ cause an accident.

3. Unjumble the jumbled word. ____________

   She tried to vcenionc the coach she was fit to play.

4. The antonym for ***vacant*** is ____________.

   empty occupied deserted

5. Add the suffix ***ly*** to these adjectives.

   bad____ soft____ glad____

6. Expand the contraction in context. ____________

   'Where's your other shoe gone?' Mum asked.

7. Write the homophone for ***flower***. ____________

8. Write the singular of ***houses***. ____________

9. Punctuate the sentence.

   the damage was not too expensive to repair and the amount was covered by insurance

10. Add commas.

    The jeep needed two new tyres both headlights replaced one indicator and a new front bumper.

11. Add one or more apostrophes.

    His parents werent happy about the damage, though they were relieved to know their son wasnt injured in the accident.

12. Circle the verb.

    The driver gave the keys back to his parents.

13. Insert the better adjective. ***embarrassed*** ***proud***

    The driver looked ____________ when he got out of the car.

14. Circle the preposition.

    The people who had gathered around the jeep cheered when the driver emerged unhurt.

15. Circle the conjunction.

    The driver looked relieved when he saw that the damage was minimal.

MY SCORE

Skill focus

Relative pronouns

Who, **which**, **that** and **whose** are words that can connect a noun to a group of words that describe it. This group of words (with a verb) is called a clause. For example:

The boy <u>who</u> sits next to me. – <u>who</u> is always used for ***people***

The <u>robot</u> that was on sale. – <u>that</u> or <u>which</u> can be used for ***things***

The woman <u>whose</u> bag was stolen. – <u>whose</u> is used to show possession by ***people and things***.

Read the short story to see how these words are used in sentences.

The thief ***who*** *stole the jewels* ***that*** *were stored in the royal palace was captured on Monday. Palace guards were led to the man,* ***whose*** *identity cannot be released, by a tracking device* ***which*** *was hidden inside the jewels.*

Practice questions

1. Circle the word that connects the noun to the words that describe it.
   The naughty boy who stole the lady's cupcake had been caught red-handed.

2. Add the words to the sentences.
   who   that   which   whose
   (a) *Alison is the girl ____________ caught him eating the treat.*
   (b) *It was the cake ____________ the lady had been saving for her morning snack.*
   (c) *The lady ____________ cupcake was stolen was very upset.*
   (d) *All that was left of the cupcake was the wrapper, ____________ was thrown in the rubbish bin.*

Day 1

1. Circle the word that connects the underlined noun to the words that describe it.
   <u>The man</u> who climbed a hill was very fit.

2. ***who*** or ***which***?
   A bird, ____________ had followed him, perched happily on a nearby tree.

3. Correct the spelling mistake. ____________
   The workers were instructed to increese their output.

4. The synonym for ***urgent*** is ____________.
   unimportant   important   trivial

5. Write ***week*** and ***weak*** in the correct places.
   'We already feel ____________ because we work so hard every ____________', the employees complained.

6. Expand the contraction in context. ____________
   I thought you'd been studying for this test.

7. Add a suffix to make the words mean ***without***.
   home______   pain______   worth______

8. Complete the simile.
   As wise as an o____________.

9. Punctuate the sentence.
   workers in some factories are expected to work in difficult and unsafe conditions

10. Add commas to enclose the extra information.
    Many clothing factories sometimes called sweatshops are located across Asia.

11. Are speech marks needed? Yes ☐ No ☐
    The boss of the factory said he'd just find other workers.

12. Write the missing verb in its correct form. ***need***
    People were worried as they ____________ the wages to live.

13. Which tense? past   present   future
    The workers will return to work tomorrow.

14. Circle the adverb.
    The new worker approached his boss nervously.

15. Exclamation ☐, command ☐ or statement ☐?
    Bring me that shirt, I want to look at it ☐

MY SCORE

Day 2

1. Circle the word that connects the underlined noun to the words that describe it.

   Dogs that chew things are not very smart.

2. ***who*** or ***whose***?

   The man ______________ shoes had been chewed by the dog was angry.

3. Rearrange the letters to make a word that means to ***sweat***.

   erpsepri ______________

4. The part of the words that means ***ten*** is ________.

   decimal decathlon decade

5. Write the homophone for ***waste***. ______________

6. Which word comes directly before ***illustrate*** in the dictionary?

   imagine illusion illness image

7. Circle two words that can be built from ***bag***.

   bagfuls upbag bagness baggage

8. Complete the simile.

   As s ______________ as a rock.

9. Punctuate the sentence.

   id really like a laptop for my birthday, rachel requested politely

10. Add a comma to make the meaning clear.

    'Bring me the paper boy!'

11. Circle the noun.

    The brand-new laptop was quite expensive.

12. ***seen*** or ***saw***?

    I ______________ this model in the catalogue!

13. Circle the verb group.

    Rachel hoped that her friends would have a great time at her party.

14. Which adverb fits best? ***happily*** ***moodily***

    The guests all chatted ______________ and noisily.

15. Circle the word that is not needed.

    Did Rachel, who felt like the luckiest girl in the world, was very happy with how the party went.

MY SCORE

Day 3

1. Circle the word that connects the underlined noun to the words that describe it.

   My flowers, which bloomed today, are lovely.

2. ***that*** or ***who***?

   Please empty the vase ______________ is filled with old flowers.

3. Correct the spelling mistake. ______________

   *Think for a moment **before** you give your arnser.*

4. The synonym for ***daring*** is ______________.

   bold boring cautious

5. ***where*** or ***wear***?

   ______________ *did you put my jacket? I want to* ______________ *it.*

6. Expand the contraction in context. ______________

   I'd never seen a bat before—it was scary!

7. Add prefixes to make the words mean the opposite.

   ______obey ______lucky

8. Complete the simile.

   As slow as a s______________.

9. Punctuate the sentence.

   the visitors to the ranch were looking forward to a sunset horseride

10. Add commas to enclose the extra information.

    The rider who was very experienced climbed onto her horse.

11. Are speech marks needed? Yes ☐ No ☐

    Head back to the ranch, the leader instructed.

12. Write the missing verb in its correct form. ***fall***

    It was a pleasant ride and fortunately no-one ______________ off their horse.

13. Which tense? past present future

    I haven't ever ridden a horse before.

14. Circle the adverb. ***quickly*** ***slowly***

    The horses ______________ galloped back to the stables.

15. Exclamation ☐, command ☐ or statement ☐?

    I enjoyed watching the sunset over the mountains ☐

MY SCORE

Day 4

1. Circle the word that connects the underlined noun to the words that describe it.

   The house whose roof collapsed will be demolished.

2. ***that*** or ***who***?

   It was next to the house ______________ has a red door.

3. Correct the spelling mistake. ______________

   The ferocious gard dog barked almost constantly.

4. The root ***bi*** in ***bicycle*** and ***biannual*** means:

   one two three

5. Write the homophone for ***alter***. ______________

6. Number the words in alphabetical order.

   normal ____ nodule ____ northern ____

7. What is the base word of ***unmanageable*** and ***mismanagement***?

   ____

8. Complete the simile.

   As s______________ as an eel.

9. Punctuate the sentence.

   do you prefer beaches enquired my best friend

10. Add a comma to make the meaning clear.

    If you can take your camera to the beach with you.

11. Circle the collective noun.

    The adults played games with a pack of cards while the children played in the water.

12. ***than*** or ***then***?

    I'd much rather go to the beach ______________ the park; ______________ we can have lunch!

13. Circle the verb group.

    You should take lessons to improve your surfing skills.

14. Circle the adverb.

    The surfer's broken board eventually washed up on the shore.

15. Which verb fits? ***struggled*** ***relaxed***

    The children ______________ and found the lessons difficult.

MY SCORE

Day 5

1. Circle the word that connects the underlined noun to the words that describe it.

   The girl whose ankle was swollen had to rest.

2. ***that*** or ***who***?

   She is the girl ______________ scored the winning goal for her netball team.

3. Correct the spelling mistake. ______________

   My older brother is very populer with all his friends.

4. A synonym for ***additional*** is ______________.

   some extra less

5. ***raise*** or ***rays***?

   The suns ______________ shone brightly through the clouds.

6. Expand the contraction in context. ______________

   He's a really great surfer, snowboarder and mountain climber.

7. Add the suffix ***ly*** to change the adjectives to adverbs.

   neat_____ loud_____ polite_____

8. Complete the simile.

   As w______________ as a ghost.

9. Punctuate the sentence.

   i wouldnt try skydiving as im afraid of heights

10. Add commas to enclose the extra information.

    My friend who is very adventurous said she would like to try it.

11. Are speech marks needed? Yes ☐ No ☐

    My brother told me that snowboarding is his favourite sport.

12. Write the missing verb in its correct form. ***try***

    I've never ______________ snowboarding but I have been skiing.

13. Which tense? past present future

    My friends were staying at the same resort.

14. Circle the adverb.

    Our family would regularly eat dinner with them.

15. Exclamation ☐, command ☐ or statement ☐?

    I'd like to go back to the same place next year ☐

MY SCORE

Skill focus

Irregular adjectives

Comparative and **superlative** adjectives are often used to compare two or more things.

This is done by adding the suffix ***er*** or ***est*** to the adjective or using the words ***more*** or ***most*** before it.

*Sean's hair is **long**. Erin's hair is **longer**. Megan's hair is the **longest**.*

*The red cupcake is **delicious**. The blue cupcake is **more delicious**. The green cupcake is the **most delicious**.*

Some adjectives are ***irregular***. This means that the entire word changes when they are used to compare two or more things. The words ***good*** and ***bad*** are two examples.

*My maths grades were **good**, my science grades were **better**, but my English grades were the **best**.*

*My handwriting is **bad**, my brother's is **worse**, but my dad's is the **worst**.*

Practice questions

1. Write the comparative and superlative forms for ***good***.

   I am getting ____________ at football, but my brother is still the ____________.

2. Write the comparative and superlative forms for ***bad***.

   I think spinach is ____________ than cabbage, but Brussels sprouts are the ____________.

Day 1

1. Write the comparative and superlative forms for ***good***.

   Joe is a ____________ skier than Sam, but Dad is the ____________.

2. Which is correct? ***smaller*** ***smallest***

   My snowman's head was ____________ than its body.

3. Rearrange the letters to make a word that means 100×10.

   dsahtuon ____________

4. The underlined word is a synonym ☐ or antonym ☐ for ***wild***?

   tame <u>savage</u> domesticated

5. Add the suffix ***ness*** to these adjectives.

   foolish______ thick______

6. The contraction ***who's*** can mean ____________ or ____________.

7. Write the homophone for ***nose***. ____________

8. Number the words in alphabetical order.

   length ____ lesson ____ layer ____ laser ____

9. Punctuate the sentence.

   what was your score out of a hundred in the science test

10. Add commas.

    In our science test we had to answer questions on planets space solids liquids and gases.

11. Add one or more apostrophes.

    Mark is very good at science and he said the test wasnt very hard, though I dont agree.

12. Circle the verb group.

    Science lessons should be both fun and informative.

13. The underlined word is an adjective ☐ or an adverb ☐?

    Our last experiment created a <u>huge</u> mess!

14. Circle the preposition.

    One child forgot to wear his safety glasses and some gooey red liquid splashed on his face!

15. ***who*** or ***whose***?

    Luckily, the child ____________ face was splashed was fine.

MY SCORE

Day 2

1. Write the comparative or superlative form for ***hard***.

   I found the mathematics test the _____________!

2. Which is correct? ***better*** ***best***

   My friend Adam got the _____________ score in the class.

3. Correct the spelling mistake. _____________

   I think I may have pulled a mussle on the trek through the forest.

4. An antonym for ***comical*** is _____________.

   funny tragic real entertaining

5. Add a prefix to make the words mean ***do again***.

   _____think _____number

6. Expand the contraction ***could've***. _____________

7. Write the homophone for ***higher***. _____________

8. Write the missing word.

   Two _____________ of scissors.

9. Punctuate the sentence.

   the poor foxs tail had become stuck in the wire fence

10. Add speech marks to show what was said.

    Look at the fox! Mimi exclaimed. Let's free it!

11. Add apostrophes for contraction or possession.

    We havent got any tools to cut its tail free but lets try our best to help it.

12. How many nouns? _____________

    On our walk we spotted a lizard, two owls, a baby possum and three rabbits.

13. The underlined words are: verb groups/ noun phrases

    Red and white spotted toadstools and lush green clumps of clover covered the forest floor.

14. Underline the adverbial of duration.

    For several hours, we wandered through the forest and admired its beauty.

15. Circle the conjunctions.

    We love to go for walks in the forest, but Dad and James prefer to stay home and watch the football.

MY SCORE

Day 3

1. Write the comparative and superlative forms for ***bad***.

   I felt _____________ than yesterday, but this is not the _____________ I have felt.

2. Which is correct? ***warm*** ***warmer***

   When you have a fever, your head feels _____________ than normal.

3. Correct the spelling mistake. _____________

   I'll need your signiture please, sir, on the line.

4. The underlined word is the synonym ☐ or antonym ☐ for ***destroy***.

   ruin restore revisit

5. Add the suffix ***ible*** to these verbs.

   digest_____ convert_____

6. The contraction ***that'd*** can mean _____________ or _____________.

7. ***eliminate*** or ***illuminate***?

   We need to win this match to _____________ that team from the league.

8. Number the words in alphabetical order.

   Friday ____ friends ____ friction ____

9. Punctuate the sentence.

   would you say youre a good swimmer

10. Add commas to the list.

    Pools lakes rivers and the ocean are all suitable places for swimming practice.

11. Add one or more apostrophes.

    Greg wasnt a very good swimmer, but he has been practising in his friend Sams pool.

12. Circle the verb group.

    Greg hopes he can swim with the Irish team.

13. Circle the pronoun and the noun it refers to.

    Mum was upset to hear Tara accidentally left her swimming costume on the bus. It was brand new!

14. Circle the preposition.

    The competitor who won the championship couldn't wipe the smile off his face.

15. Circle the conjunction.

    Because the sun was out in force, the children were continually reminded to apply suncream.

MY SCORE

WEEK 21

Day 4

1. Write the comparative or superlative form for ***scary***.

   The film we watched was the ____________ I had ever seen.

2. Which is correct? ***worse*** ***worst***

   I had the ____________ nightmares that night.

3. Correct the spelling mistake. ____________

   She hadn't seen her cousin in years and she almost didn't reconise him.

4. A synonym for ***immature*** is ____________.

   childish grown-up mature

5. Add a prefix to make the words mean ***not***.

   _____certain _____kind _____happy

6. Expand the contraction ***should've***. ____________

7. Write the homophone for ***pause***. ____________

8. One deer. Two ____________.

9. Punctuate the sentence.

   family members travelled from far and wide to be at the annual browns family reunion

10. Add speech marks to show what was said.

    Wow! Look how much you've grown! Aunt Mavis exclaimed.

11. Add an apostrophe for contraction or possession.

    Uncle Johns voice boomed across the hall.

12. How many nouns? ____________

    I had not seen my cousins for two years and they had bought me a gift.

13. Write the missing pronoun.

    ____________ had come all the way from Canada with their mum and dad.

14. Circle the preposition.

    We held the family reunion at our local park.

15. Write the better conjunction. ***Because*** ***Although***

    ____________ I had a great time at the reunion, I was very tired after all of the chatting and eating!

Day 5

1. Write the comparative and superlative forms for ***good***.

   I think that apples taste ____________ than oranges, but bananas taste the ____________.

2. Which is correct? ***tasty*** ***tastiest***

   This is the ____________ fruit salad I have eaten.

3. Rearrange the letters to make a word that means to ***take hold of something by force***.

   eizse ____________

4. The antonym for ***gigantic*** is ____________.

   minuscule enormous generous

5. Add the suffix ***ous*** to change the nouns to adjectives.

   fame_____ fibre_____

6. The contraction ***she'd*** can mean ____________ or ____________.

7. ***higher*** or ***hire***?

   We need to climb ____________!

8. The underlined word comes first in alphabetical order. Yes ☐ No ☐

   justice <u>jungle</u> junk judge

9. Punctuate the sentence.

   historically pirates were known for burying their treasure to keep it safe

10. Add commas to the list.

    The pirate gathered his rusty compass his trusty parrot the crumpled map and his telescope.

11. Add one or more apostrophes.

    The pirates ship wasnt in the best shape—it was very old and rickety.

12. Circle the verb group.

    The crew were hoping for a share of the treasure.

13. Circle the adjectives.

    The wicked pirate had a sinister crew.

14. Circle the preposition.

    The pirate's parrot, called Horace, was perched happily on his shoulder.

15. ***who*** or ***that***?

    The crew members ____________ were tired retired to their hammocks for the night.

MY SCORE

Possessive determiners

There is a group of words that are often used before nouns to give the reader or listener more precise information. Some of these words include:

my your his her its our your their

These words can be used before a noun to tell others who it belongs to. For example:

This is ***my hat****. That is* ***his hat****. Here is* ***her hat****. Where is* ***your hat****?*

The underlined words show that each hat (noun) belongs to a different person.

Sometimes, these words are often confused with their homophones. For example:

your/you're (you are)

their/there (a place)/they're (they are)

its/it's (it is)

Choosing the incorrect word can change the meaning of your sentence, so remember to think carefully about which one you choose.

Practice questions

1. Circle the word used to tell who the underlined noun belongs to.
   The captain carefully navigated his ship towards the dock.

2. ***its*** or ***it's***?
   Once ______________ contents had been unloaded, the ship was refuelled and reloaded.

---

1. Circle the word used to tell who the underlined noun belongs to.
   This year, we will be going to the USA for our holiday.

2. ***its*** or ***it's***?
   The USA is known for ______________ film and music industries.

3. Correct the spelling mistake. ______________
   The hite of the tallest building in the city was impressive.

4. Add prefixes to make the words mean ***not***.
   ______possible ______regular

5. Write ***weather*** and ***whether*** in the correct places.
   Do you know ______________ the ______________ will be warm tomorrow?

6. Which word comes directly before ***computer*** in alphabetical order?
   cost collect contain cold

7. Circle two words that can be built from ***fire***.
   backfired fireness fireside firely

8. One batch. Two ______________.

9. Punctuate the sentence.
   do you know which city the worlds tallest building is in

10. Write the correct form of ***tall*** in the sentence.
    The Empire State Building in New York City was once the ______________ building in the world.

11. Insert the best collective noun. ***choir band***
    There was a ______________ of musicians playing on the bridge.

12. Circle the proper nouns.
    If you visit New York, you must see the Statue of Liberty, and should visit Central Park, too.

13. Circle the pronouns.
    Dad was proud of himself when he sang karaoke.

14. Circle the adverbs.
    Tourists took photos hastily as the bus slowly drove by each attraction.

15. Circle the preposition.
    Walking across the Brooklyn Bridge was unforgettable.

Day 2

1. Circle the word used to tell who the underlined noun belongs to.

   Michelle has invited me to her party.

2. ***their*** or ***they're***?

   Michelle and her twin, Megan, will be celebrating ______________ birthday at the beach.

3. Rearrange the letters to make a word that means a ***dress-up outfit***.

   mectuso ______________

4. The root ***dent*** as in ***dentist*** and ***denture*** means:

   foot tooth doctor

5. ***heard*** or ***herd***?

   I haven't ______________ this song before.

6. The underlined word comes first in alphabetical order. Yes ☐ No ☐

   phone photo phoney phobia

7. What is the base word of ***treatment*** and ***mistreated***? ______________

8. The underlined word is the synonym ☐ or antonym ☐ for ***gloomy***?

   cheery depressing exciting

9. Add a comma to clarify meaning.

   While I was thinking the cat walked into the room.

10. Write the correct form of ***good*** in the sentence.

    It would be good to dress up as Batman but it would be ______________ to dress up as Spiderman.

11. Circle the abstract noun.

    I got a fright when I saw her ghost costume.

12. Circle the nouns.

    There were witches, ghosts, vampires and even a clown at the party.

13. Write ***may*** or ***should***.

    I ______________ have chosen a scarier costume—no-one was afraid of Spiderman!

14. Circle the conjunction.

    The judges couldn't decide on the best costume, so they asked the guests to vote for their favourite.

15. Circle the preposition.

    During the party, I made many new friends.

MY SCORE

Day 3

1. Circle the word used to tell who the underlined noun belongs to.

   My dad left his jacket on the bus.

2. ***your*** or ***you're***?

   'Do you know which ______________ bus was?' asked the employee at the bus station.

3. Correct the spelling mistake. ______________

   A bus driver looked for the jackit.

4. Add the suffix ***en*** to these adjectives.

   light______ sweet______

5. Write the homophone for ***allowed***. ______________

6. Expand the contraction in context. ______________

   I thought she'd make it to the meeting on time.

7. Circle three words that can be built from ***eat***.

   uneaten re-eat ate eated edible

8. One sheep. Two ______________.

9. Punctuate the sentence.

   is the jacket black asked the bus driver

10. ***who*** or ***whose***?

    The man ______________ lost his jacket spoke to the bus driver.

11. Circle the simile.

    The jacket is as soft as velvet.

12. Circle the adjectives.

    The observant bus driver soon found the leather jacket.

13. Circle the verb groups.

    Dad must have been distracted by his phone, which is why he forgot his jacket.

14. Write the conjunction. ***but*** ***so***

    Dad will always be more careful in future, ______________ he doesn't lose anything else.

15. Insert a question word.

    ______________ you know of anyone else who has left their belongings on a bus or train?

WEEK 22

Day 4

1. Circle the word used to tell who the underlined noun belongs to.

   I went on the train to the city with my <u>family</u>.

2. ***their*** or ***they're***?

   The passengers bought ____________ tickets before they boarded the train.

3. Correct the spelling mistake. ____________

   What you're wearing isn't sootable for this establishment.

4. The part of the words that means ***bend*** is ________.

   reflex flexible inflexibility

5. ***current*** or ***currant***?

   Would you like a ____________ bun?

6. Expand the contraction in context. ____________

   When's the best time to call you?

7. What is the base word of ***outline*** and ***linear***?

   ____

8. The underlined word is a synonym ☐ or antonym ☐ for ***trivial***.

   crucial <u>unimportant</u> important

9. Punctuate the sentence.

   do you think this palace cost a lot of money to build

10. ***who*** or ***whose***?

    The prince gave a speech to the people, ____________ listened intently.

11. Circle the simile.

    The princess was as graceful as a ballerina.

12. Circle the adjectives.

    Her elegant dress and sparkling crown were beautiful.

13. Write the missing verb in its correct form. ***bring***

    Have you ____________ your camera with you?

14. Circle the adverbs.

    We had sadly forgotten our camera as we had already left home.

15. Is the word ***reign*** used correctly? Yes ☐ No ☐

    There was a reign of terror when the cruel king took control.

MY SCORE

Day 5

1. Circle the word used to tell who the underlined noun belongs to.

   You must make sure your <u>home</u> is secure during a tornado.

2. ***your*** or ***you're***?

   Have you put all ____________ belongings in a safe place?

3. Correct the spelling mistake. ____________

   A distructive tornado destroyed many homes and businesses.

4. Add prefixes to make the words mean the opposite.

   ____familiar ____polite

5. Write the homophone for ***no***. ____________

6. Expand the contraction in context. ____________

   Who's coming to the picnic with us?

7. Circle two words that can be built from ***explode***.

   explosive explosion re-explode

8. One tooth. Two ____________.

9. Add a comma to enclose the extra information.

   Natural disasters like tornadoes are common in the United States of America.

10. ***whose*** or ***who***?

    A woman ____________ dog went missing during the tornado was very upset.

11. Write the missing pronoun.

    Our garden was a mess and ____________ had to work together to clean it up.

12. Circle the nouns.

    Fortunately, the tornado did not damage many homes or buildings.

13. Write the missing verb in its correct form. ***sweep***

    Dad ____________ the deck while I raked the leaves.

14. Circle the adverb.

    As we were working, my brother shouted excitedly, 'Look what I found!'

15. Circle the preposition.

    We were astonished to find the lady's dog hiding behind a tree.

MY SCORE

Skill focus

Plurals made from compound words

Plural is a word used to indicate more than one.

There are many ways to form the plural of a word.

To form the plural of most nouns, we add *s* or *es* to the end of the word.

Sometimes, two or more words are joined together to form **compound nouns**.

Compound nouns may or may not have a space between the connected nouns, or they may be joined with a hyphen (-). For example:

super + market = supermarket

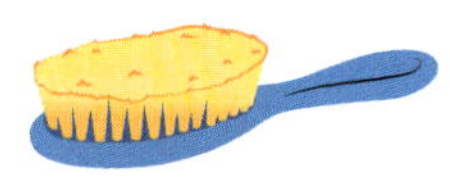

hair + brush = hairbrush

sister + in + law = sister-in-law

ice + cream = ice cream

To make a plural of a compound noun, we usually add ***s*** or ***es*** to the end of the word, or the most important noun. For example:

supermarkets **hairbrushes** **sisters**-in-law ice **creams**

Practice questions

1. Make these words plural.
   (a) *football* ____________
   (b) *lawnmower* ____________
   (c) *looker-on* ____________
   (d) *father-in-law* ____________

Day 1

1. Write the plural of ***butterfly***. ____________
2. Add the plural to the sentence. ***cupful***
   My recipe needs three ____________ of flour.
3. Rearrange the letters to make a word that means a ***plan*** or ***timetable***.
   ldehsuce ____________
4. The antonym for ***vague*** is ____________.
   connected clear spiteful harsh
5. Add the suffix ***able*** to these verbs.
   teach______ notice______
6. Expand the contraction in context. ____________
   'What's your mother already told you?' Dad warned.
7. Write the homophone for ***choose***. ____________
8. Punctuate the sentence.
   which newspaper do you like to read we were asked
9. Add apostrophe(s).
   Newspapers arent as popular as they once were.
10. Circle the verb group
    Computers, tablets and e-readers might replace many books, magazines and newspapers one day.
11. Circle the nouns.
    My dad still buys the newspaper every Saturday.
12. Rewrite in the simple present tense.
    We bought the paper. ____________
13. Write the comparative or superlative form: ***interesting***
    I find this article ____________ than that one.
14. Which verb better expresses the meaning—***skimmed*** or ***examined***?
    She quickly ____________ through the paper.
15. Add the pronoun.
    Dad likes to read the newspaper by ____________.

Day 2

1. Write the plural of ***runner-up***. ____________
2. Add the plural to the sentence. ***push-up***

   The coach made the whole team do twenty ____________.

3. Correct the spelling mistake. ____________

   We watched the lightining from our window.

4. A synonym for ***obvious*** is ____________.

   correct apparent different

5. Add prefixes to make the words mean the opposite.

   _____loyal _____pronounce

6. Expand the contraction in context. ____________

   When's the train due to arrive at the station?

7. ***except*** or ***accept***?

   I like all animals ____________ for snakes because they frighten me.

8. Punctuate the sentence.

   a huge variety of flowers was growing including buttercups roses tulips and daffodils

9. Add speech marks to show what was said.

   Wow! Fin exclaimed. Look at all the colourful flowers!

10. Circle the verb group.

    When it's sunny, many visitors come to see the flowers and to eat lunch in the café.

11. Circle the pronoun and the noun it refers to.

    When the drivers arrive to take flowers to the florists, they have to wait for their vans to be loaded.

12. Are speech marks needed? Yes ☐ No ☐

    The driver said the time spent waiting was annoying.

13. ***they're*** or ***their***?

    The workers have ____________ lunch at 1 p.m.

14. Write the missing verb in its correct form. ***cut***

    Workers must wear gloves when they are ____________ the flowers.

15. Exclamation ☐, command ☐ or statement ☐?

    I can't believe how many roses we are selling ☐

MY SCORE

Day 3

1. Write the plural of ***eleven-year-old***. ____________
2. Add the plural to the sentence. ***brother-in-law***

   My mum has two ____________.

3. Correct the spelling mistake. ____________

   We purchased an expensive pirfume from the shop.

4. The underlined word is a synonym ☐ or antonym ☐ for ***offend***?

   please upset delight insult

5. Add the suffix ***ful*** to these nouns.

   forget_____ cheer_____ waste_____

6. Expand the contraction in context. ____________

   I thought he'd already brushed his teeth.

7. Write the homophone for ***sell***. ____________
8. Punctuate the sentence.

   whats your favourite reality cooking show on television

9. Add one or more apostrophes.

   The guests on the show werent impressed with the starter; one mans face showed his disgust.

10. Write ***in*** or ***with***.

    One contestant, specialising ____________ desserts, was reduced to tears during the show.

11. Circle the pronoun and the noun it refers to.

    Dad thinks he could do better than some of the contestants.

12. Rewrite in the simple past tense.

    We will gather at 7 pm to watch the show.

    ____

13. Write the comparative or superlative form. ***bad***

    The new host was ____________ than the previous one.

14. Circle the verb group.

    A difficult challenge the contestants faced was catering for a group of teenagers.

15. The underlined words mean? ***exploded*** ***kicked***

    One contestant accidentally blew up the microwave.

MY SCORE

WEEK 23

WEEK 23

Day 4

1. Write the plural of ***bird-of-prey***. ______________
2. Add the plural to the sentence. ***passer-by***
   None of the ______________ offered to help the elderly gentleman.
3. Unjumble the jumbled word. ______________
   Areas close to the equator experience high velles of humidity.
4. The synonym for ***peculiar*** is ______________.
   strange normal enough
5. Add prefixes to make the words mean the opposite.
   ______complete ______decided
6. Expand the contraction in context. ______________
   What has been decided since I've been away?
7. ***pair*** or ***pear***?
   Someone's left a ______________ of shoes behind.
8. Punctuate the sentences.
   in south america three countries are on the equator they are ecuador colombia and brazil
9. Add speech marks to show what was said.
   My mum said, Most countries near the equator have warm, humid weather all year.
10. Write ***one*** or ***the***.
    Indonesia, which is made up of over 17 000 islands, is ______________ country located on the equator.
11. Circle four nouns.
    The wet season, which usually lasts for about six months, brings torrential rains to the region.
12. Are speech marks needed? Yes ☐ No ☐
    We crossed the equator on a cruise ship, my friend shared.
13. ***breath*** or ***breathe***?
    When it is very humid it sometimes feels hard to ______________ properly.
14. Write the missing verb in its correct form. ***find***
    We ______________ out many facts about the equator for our project.
15. Exclamation ☐, command ☐ or question ☐?
    You must finish your project by tomorrow ☐

MY SCORE

Day 5

1. Write the plural of ***high school***. ______________
2. Add the plural to this sentence. ***maid of honour***
   The ______________ led the bride down the aisle.
3. Rearrange the letters to make a word that means ***erase*** or ***remove***.
   telede ______________
4. The synonym for ***persuade*** is ______________.
   complain convince force
5. Add the suffix ***ly*** to these adjectives.
   happy______ sweet______ quiet______
6. Expand the contraction in context. ______________
   Who's got a sandwich for lunch today?
7. Write the homophone for ***mane***. ______________
8. Punctuate the sentence.
   the disgusted children didnt want to dissect the frog in their science class
9. Add one or more apostrophes.
   Scientists discoveries continue to improve the lives of humans everywhere.
10. ***isn't*** or ***aren't***?
    We ______________ supposed to be in the lab without an adult present.
11. Circle the nouns.
    The children were told to tidy up the lab.
12. Rewrite in the simple present tense.
    I enjoyed science classes.
    ____
13. Write the comparative or superlative form: ***large***
    Our tomatoes, which were the ______________ in the class, tasted delicious.
14. Which verb better expresses the meaning—***advanced*** or ***waited***?
    The excited children ______________ eagerly for the experiment to begin.
15. Circle the word that does not belong.
    One classroom, which is sometimes in the older part of the school, isn't suitable for science.

Day 1

1. Rearrange the letters to make a word that means to ***hurt*** or ***harm***.

   dnwuo ____________

2. Write the plural of ***football***. ____________

3. ***sight*** or ***site***?

   The harbour is a popular tourist ____________.

4. The synonym for ***sweet*** is ____________.

   bitter nasty nice

5. The base word of ***historical*** is ____________.

6. Which word comes directly before ***magic*** in alphabetical order?

   machine magazine mad

7. Punctuate the sentence.

   my dad plays in a band with two guitar players a drummer and a lead singer

8. Add speech marks to show what was said.

   Whose house are you practising at tonight? I asked Dad.

9. Add commas to enclose the additional information.

   Dad said our garage which is very large was the best place to practise.

10. ***seen*** or ***saw***?

    I have never ____________ my dad perform on stage.

11. Add the superlative form of ***good***.

    My dad's friend Mick is the ____________ singer I have ever heard.

12. ***who*** or ***that***?

    Mick's daughter is a girl ____________ I go to school with.

13. Write ***do*** or ***does***.

    Which instument ____________ your dad play?

14. Circle the preposition.

    Dad's drumkit was already in the garage.

15. Insert two full stops.

    The other members of Dad's band arrived after dinner they practised until it was almost midnight

Day 2

1. Rearrange the letters to make a word that means to be ***inquisitive and interested***.

   crusiuo ____________

2. Write the singular of ***brushes***. ____________

3. ***their*** or ***they're***?

   Do you know if ____________ coming?

4. The antonym for ***terrible*** is ____________.

   wonderful appalling awful

5. Circle two words that can be built from ***hurt***.

   hurtful yoghurt unhurt hurtling

6. The underlined word comes first in alphabetical order. Yes ☐ No ☐

   wallet walk wake <u>waiter</u>

7. Punctuate the sentence.

   my brother james who is only four years old is an excellent artist

8. Add one or more apostrophes.

   We didnt know about James art skills until one day he got into my sisters art supplies.

9. Add commas.

   James enjoys creating different artworks using paints pencils crayons and collage with scrap materials.

10. ***was*** or ***were***?

    We ____________ amazed when we first saw some of James' drawings.

11. Circle the adverbs.

    Many artists work creatively and methodically with materials they choose.

12. Circle the adjectives.

    The neatly hung artworks were vibrant and unique.

13. Which tense? past present future

    We will be visiting the Louvre Museum in France next year.

14. Circle the word used to tell who the underlined noun belongs to.

    James and I have been learning all about famous artists on our <u>computer</u> at home.

15. Is the word ***restored*** used correctly? Yes ☐ No ☐

    Many old artworks are restored by professional artists.

MY SCORE

WEEK 24

Day 3

1. Rearrange the letters to make a word that means to ***buy something***.

   scphurae ______________

2. Write the plural of ***mess***. ______________

3. ***steel*** or ***steal***?

   You mustn't ______________, it's against the law.

4. The synonym for ***empty*** is ______________.

   filled loaded vacant

5. What is the base word of ***unforgettable*** and ***forgotten***? ______________

6. Which word comes directly after ***salad*** in alphabetical order?

   salt sale same

7. Punctuate the sentence.

   mr higgins who lives next door is old and frail

8. Add speech marks to show what was said.

   How are you today boys? asked Mr Higgins as we rode past his house on our way home from school.

9. Add commas to clarify meaning.

   When he saw Mr Higgins trying to mow my brother stopped to ask if he needed any help.

10. ***Your*** or ***You're***?

    '______________ very kind to offer', replied Mr Higgins with a friendly smile.

11. Add the comparative form of ***bad***.

    Mr Higgins told us that his arthritis was getting ______________ in his old age.

12. ***who*** or ***that***?

    Mr Higgins' son, ______________ lives a short distance away, would be visiting in the afternoon to help with the gardening.

13. ***a*** or ***an***?

    We helped Mr Higgins for about ______________ hour before his son arrived.

14. Circle the adverbs.

    Mr Higgins warmly thanked us for our hard work and quickly gave us a cold drink for our effort.

15. Insert two full stops.

    Mr Higgins was very pleased with his new garden he suggested we visit again for afternoon tea

MY SCORE

Day 4

1. Rearrange the letters to make a word that means a ***young person or teenager***.

   hutyo ______________

2. Write the singular of ***horses***. ______________

3. ***their*** or ***there***?

   Have they got ______________ tickets?

4. The antonym for ***various*** is ______________.

   several few assorted

5. The base word of ***geographical*** is ______________.

6. The underlined word comes first in alphabetical order. Yes ☐ No ☐

   objective <u>object</u> objection

7. Punctuate the sentence.

   at the same time every year my parents friends and their families go on a camping holiday

8. Add one or more apostrophes.

   The mens faces were red from setting up the tents.

9. Add commas.

   While our dads were setting up the tents all the children changed into their swimsuits grabbed a towel and went to the lake for a swim.

10. Which is correct?

    men's families *mens' families*

11. Rewrite in the simple past tense (one verb).

    Our mums were taking photos.

    ____

12. Circle the preposition.

    My best friend Megan swam beside me.

13. Rewrite in the simple present tense.

    The water was very cool and calm.

    ____

14. Circle the word used to tell who the underlined noun belongs to.

    After a long day of swimming, we ate our <u>dinner</u> quickly and then went to bed.

15. Is the word ***lush*** used correctly? Yes ☐ No ☐

    We slept contently surrounded by the lush forest.

MY SCORE

Day 5

1. Rearrange the letters to make a word that means ***upset, worried and tense***.

   saxuoin ____________

2. Write the plural of ***merry-go-round***. ____________

3. ***red*** or ***read***?

   Have you ____________ that book?

4. The synonym for ***unlikely*** is ____________.

   possible   improbable   believable

5. Circle four words that can be built from ***be***.

   was   is   can   have   are   were

6. Which word comes directly after ***calculator*** in alphabetical order?

   call   calendar   calf

7. Punctuate the sentence.

   did you know that lack of sleep causes tiredness yawning bad temper and lack of concentration

8. Add speech marks to show what was said.

   I think that explains why you're always so grumpy! Dad told my brother with a chuckle.

9. Add commas to enclose the additional information.

   My brother who is only twelve stays up to midnight playing video games.

10. Which is correct?

    both parents' rules   *both parent's rules*

11. Add the comparative and superlative forms of ***bad***.

    My brother's sleeping habits are usually ____________ at weekends, but school holidays are the ____________.

12. ***who*** or ***that***?

    The gaming console ____________ my brother is obsessed with is getting very old.

13. Write ***its*** or ***it's***.

    Mum has told him that once ____________ broken, he will not be getting a new one.

14. Circle the prepositions.

    My brother locks the game controller inside his drawer, so I can't play it when he's not at home.

15. Circle the error.

    I think playing too many video games is a incredible waste of time.

Skill focus review

1. Correct the spelling mistake. ____________

   Do you know your neighbor across the road?

2. A synonym for ***magnificent*** is ____________.

   unattractive   glorious   plain

3. Add prefixes to make the words mean the opposite.

   ____possible   ____responsible

4. Expand the contraction in context. ____________

   You'd have liked the film, it was really funny!

5. Write the homophone for ***serial***. ____________

6. Write the plural of ***runner-up***. ____________

7. Complete the simile.

   As cl____________ as a bell.

8. Add a comma to enclose the additional information.

   Exotic animals such as zebras and lions can be seen on the African continent.

9. Circle the word used to tell who the underlined noun belongs to.

   The dangerous black mamba uses its powerful venom to capture its <u>prey</u>.

10. Add ***its*** or ***it's***.

    The snake slithered on ____________ stomach along the dusty ground.

11. Circle the word that connects the noun in bold to the words that give more information about it.

    *The guide showed us **the animals** that were at the watering hole.*

12. ***who*** or ***whose***?

    There was a lady on our tour ____________ took a lot of photos.

13. Circle the verb groups.

    People must be careful around waterways in Africa, as crocodiles can attack at any time.

14. Add the helping verb that shows a stronger obligation.   ***must***   ***should***

    People ____________ also be wary of elephants and buffalo as they can be dangerous.

15. Add the superlative form of ***good***.

    Our trip to Africa was the ____________ holiday that I have ever been on.

MY SCORE

WEEK 24

Skill focus

Idioms

An **idiom** is a phrase whose meaning is not related to its individual words. For example:

Idiom: in hot water	Idiom: looking green around the gills	Idiom: come clean
Actual meaning: to be in trouble	Actual meaning: looking unwell	Actual meaning: to tell the truth

Using figures of speech like idioms in your writing helps you share meaning in an interesting way.

Practice questions

1. Circle the idiom (common expression).
   The magician vanished in the blink of an eye and everyone was amazed.
2. The idiom above means:
   the magician vanished quickly. ☐
   the magician closed his eyes. ☐

Day 1

1. Circle the idiom (common expression).
   I was scared but I knew it was time to face the music.
2. The idiom above means to:
   be brave. ☐ *listen to music.* ☐
3. Correct the spelling mistake. __________
   The child was asked to translait for her parents, as they couldn't speak English.
4. The part of the words that means ***bend*** is __________.
   reflex flexible inflexibility
5. Write ***won*** and ***one*** in the correct places.
   __________ *of the girls who* __________ *an award had her picture in the local newspaper.*
6. Which word comes directly before ***service*** in the dictionary?
   sermon serve serpent serious
7. Circle two words that can be built from ***break***.
   breaked break-up breaken unbroken
8. Write the plural of ***berry***. __________
9. Punctuate the sentence.
   becoming fluent in another language requires many years of practice
10. Add one or more apostrophes.
    Its useful to learn to say some basics in other languages when travelling overseas.
11. Are speech marks needed? Yes ☐ No ☐
    Which foreign languages are taught at your school? he asked.
12. ***shore*** or ***sure***?
    Are you __________ *that's how you say it?*
13. Which tense? past present future
    My grandparents spoke Italian and French.
14. Circle the word used to tell who the underlined noun belongs to.
    I've been learning Japanese at my <u>school</u> for three years.
15. ***who*** or ***that***?
    There is a lady in my street __________ *spent many years studying in Japan.*

MY SCORE

Day 2

1. Circle the idiom (common expression).

   I got into hot water when I lost my mum's favourite necklace.

2. The idiom above means to:

   take a bath. ☐ *be in trouble.* ☐

3. Rearrange the letters to make a word that means to ***fight or disagree***.

   gaure ____________

4. The antonym for ***gratitude*** is ____________.

   ingratitude thankfulness appreciation

5. ***mist*** or ***missed***?

   Because of the morning ____________ we were running late and ____________ the ferry.

6. Number the words in alphabetical order.

   noisy ____ nomadic ____ nocturnal ____

7. What is the base word of ***celebratory*** and ***uncelebrated***? ____________

8. ***loose*** or ***lose***?

   Are you absolutely certain you didn't just ____________ it somewhere?

9. Punctuate the sentence.

   i havent studied ancient civilisations before because they dont interest me

10. Add a comma to clarify meaning.

    Ancient Egyptians worshipped many animals built impressive pyramids and invented many things.

11. Circle the proper nouns.

    Leaders of Ancient Egypt were referred to as Pharaohs.

12. ***rain*** or ***reign***?

    Cleopatra was the last pharaoh to ____________ over the people of Egypt.

13. Circle the verb.

    The children learned a lot during their museum visit.

14. Which adverb fits better? ***actively*** ***unwillingly***

    The eager children ____________ searched for information.

15. ***who*** or ***that***?

    A boy ____________ is in my class said he'd like to be an archaeologist.

MY SCORE

Day 3

1. Circle the idiom (common expression).

   This is a secret so you can't let the cat out of the bag.

2. The idiom above means to:

   give away the secret. ☐ *put the cat outside.* ☐

3. Correct the spelling mistake. ____________

   My temperature was taken with the themomater.

4. The synonym for ***optimistic*** is ____________.

   doubtful hopeful precise

5. Write the homophone for ***site***. ____________

6. Expand the contraction in context. ____________

   I think he's going to fail his exams.

7. Add the suffix ***less*** to these words.

   sleep____ fear____ beard____

8. Write the singular of ***summaries***. ____________

9. Punctuate the sentence.

   if a persons body temperature becomes too high or low there can be serious health risks

10. Add one or more apostrophes.

    The childs temperature wasnt in the normal range, so she was admitted for treatment.

11. Add speech marks to show what was said.

    The nurse explained, Close to 37 °C is a normal, healthy temperature.

12. ***two*** or ***too***?

    The observant doctor spotted ____________ tiny marks on the girl's ankle.

13. Write the missing verb in its correct form. ***bite***

    The doctor guessed she had been ____________ by a rare breed of spider.

14. Circle the word used to tell who the underlined noun belongs to.

    The doctor told the lady that her <u>daughter</u> would be fine.

15. Is ***administered*** used correctly? Yes ☐ No ☐

    The antibiotic, which was administered quickly, saved the girl's life.

WEEK 25

Day 4

1. Circle the idiom (common expression).
   I am at a loose end because I don't know what to do.
2. The idiom above means:
   to have nothing to do. ☐
   needing to tie your shoelaces. ☐
3. Correct the spelling mistake. ____________
   Is the information you found ackurate?
4. The antonym for ***plentiful*** is ____________.
   enough scarce wealthy
5. Write the homophone for ***right***. ____________
6. Expand the contraction in context. ____________
   When's the bus supposed to be coming?
7. Add the suffix ***ly*** to these words.
   rude____ safe____ swift____
8. ***brought*** or ***bought***?
   Have you ____________ over the new clothes you ____________ to show us?
9. Punctuate the sentence.
   do you have any hobbies she asked me
10. Add commas.
    The friendly fast-talking and bubbly woman showed us her large well-organised and tidy office.
11. The underlined words are: noun phrases/ verb groups
    The woman had been giving <u>scrapbooking lessons</u> for <u>two years</u>.
12. ***seen*** or ***scene***?
    One of the pages in the book recreated a beautiful beach ____________.
13. Which tense? past present future
    They will attend classes for eight weeks.
14. Which verb fits? ***mumbled*** ***chatted***
    They ____________ happily as they worked on their books.
15. Is the word ***obsession*** used correctly?
    Yes ☐ No ☐
    Stamp collecting has become an obsession for that woman.

MY SCORE

Day 5

1. Circle the idiom (common expression).
   Will you tell me exactly what you mean and don't beat around the bush.
2. The idiom above means to:
   go for a hike. ☐
   avoid saying what you mean. ☐
3. Correct the spelling mistake. ____________
   The astronaut heading the space misshun was formerly a jet pilot.
4. A synonym for ***optional*** is ____________.
   compulsory voluntary forbidden
5. Write the homophone for ***hour***. ____________
6. Expand the contraction in context. ____________
   It's going to be very hot tomorrow.
7. Add prefixes to make the words mean the opposite.
   ____agree ____obey
8. Write the plural of ***pharmacy***. ____________
9. Punctuate the sentence.
   the shuttle launch wasnt broadcast on television until the following day
10. Add one or more apostrophes.
    Space doesnt really interest me, and besides, I dont think itll ever be affordable to travel there.
11. Are speech marks needed? Yes ☐ No ☐
    Gran said that she remembers watching the moon landing in 1969.
12. ***foreword*** or ***forward***?
    Neil Armstrong bounced ____________ on the moon's surface.
13. Write the missing verb in its correct form. ***watch***
    'It was a moment in time when the whole world seemed to be ____________', Mum explained.
14. Circle the word used to tell who the underlined noun belongs to.
    He was also joined by his <u>colleague</u>, Buzz Aldrin.
15. Write ***before*** or ***since***.
    The moon, which has been walked on by 12 people in total, hasn't been visited ____________ 1972.

MY SCORE

Proper adjectives

Adjectives are words used to describe nouns or pronouns, making writing clearer and more interesting. For example:

*The **old**, **bent**, **gnarled** tree swayed in the **strong** breeze.*

These are called **common adjectives**.

Proper adjectives are also used to describe nouns or pronouns, but they are made using proper nouns. For example:

(Proper noun)

*This rose is from **Japan**. The **Japanese** rose is beautiful.*

(Proper adjective)

Proper adjectives are usually used to describe where a person or object comes from.

They always start with a capital letter.

Practice questions

1. Circle the proper adjective.

   Many excellent British actors have starred in popular films.

2. Are the underlined words proper adjectives?

   Yes ☐ No ☐

   Daniel Radcliffe is a British actor who starred in the Harry Potter films.

1. Circle the proper adjective.

   Whales can sometimes be seen along the Australian coastline.

2. The underlined word is a proper adjective ☐ or proper noun ☐?

   The Indian tourists watched the whales from Dunsborough.

3. Rearrange the letters to make a word that means a ***bad dream***.

   reamhgitn ______________

4. The underlined word is a synonym ☐ or antonym ☐ for ***preserve***?

   destroy keep catch

5. Write the homophone for ***great***. ______________

6. Expand the contraction in context. ______________

   It's been very hot now for a whole week!

7. Add the suffix ***ness*** to these adjectives.

   sad____ great____

8. Write the missing word. ***flock*** ***herd***

   A ______________ of sheep.

9. Punctuate the sentence.

   have you ever had the same dream more than once

10. Add commas.

    People can have nightmares about being chased losing their teeth falling being lost and many other things.

11. Add one or more apostrophes.

    The childs cries didnt wake her parents, so they werent there to comfort her when she woke up from her bad dream.

12. Underline the noun phrases.

    The small puppy was whimpering as it slept on the broken old chair.

13. Write ***they're*** or ***their***.

    Some people can fly in ______________ dreams.

14. Insert a pronoun.

    When I am having a bad dream, I try to pinch ______________ so I will wake up.

15. Insert a question word.

    ______________ time did you go to bed last night?

MY SCORE

WEEK 26

Day 2

1. Circle the proper adjective.

   Mr Tan, who was a former winner of the national baking contest, was an Italian chef.

2. Are the underlined words proper adjectives?
   Yes ☐ No ☐

   The Italian chef was renowned for his extravagant French pastries.

3. Correct the spelling mistake. ____________

   An enormus parcel arrived today.

4. An antonym for ***plausible*** is ____________.

   real unbelievable funny generous

5. Write the homophone for ***ewe***. ____________

6. Expand the contraction in context. ____________

   I'd forgotten to bring my homework to school.

7. Add a prefix to make the words mean ***do again***.

   ____paint ____load ____heat

8. ***who is*** or ***who has***?

   My granny, ____________ written me a letter every week since I was five, is in hospital at the moment.

9. Punctuate the sentence.

   whats the busiest time of year for the postal service

10. Add speech marks to show what was said.

    He answered, The Christmas season is very busy.

11. Add apostrophes for contraction or possession.

    I havent received any letters recently, but Dads always getting lots.

12. How many adjectives? ____________

    A large parcel arrived on the front doorstep on Monday.

13. Circle the idiom (common expression).

    Dad said that the delivery fee had cost him an arm and a leg.

14. Circle the pronoun.

    He ordered the book online using his computer.

15. Circle the adverbs.

    Dad rarely gets excited, but he accidentally tripped when he ran quickly to collect his parcel.

MY SCORE

Day 3

1. Circle the proper adjective.

   The taxi driver, who is French, warmly greeted us before starting our journey.

2. The underlined word is a proper adjective ☐ or proper noun ☐?

   He asked if we were Swedish, but we told him we came from Scotland.

3. Rearrange ***qatuore*** to make a word that means an imaginary line around Earth.

   ____

4. The underlined word is the synonym ☐ or antonym ☐ for ***clear***?

   murky transparent opaque

5. ***aloud*** or ***allowed***?

   You will not be ____________ to leave the country unless you find that passport.

6. Number the words in alphabetical order.

   support ____ supply ____ suppose ____

7. Add the suffix ***er*** to these verbs.

   teach____ explore____ rob____

8. ***that had*** or ***that would***?

   I think ____________ be a great idea.

9. Punctuate the sentence.

   my dads passport has stamps from many countries

10. Add commas.

    Last year our family visited China New Zealand Colombia South Africa and Indonesia.

11. Is an apostrophe needed? Yes ☐ No ☐

    The girls in the line were chatting.

12. Write ***congested*** or ***digested***.

    The ____________ traffic on the road was bad.

13. ***it's*** or ***its***?

    When ____________ time for the flight, make sure your bag has ____________ tag attached, so it doesn't get lost.

14. Circle the noun the underlined pronoun refers to.

    Dad says I should travel as much as he did.

15. Underline the adverbial of duration.

    Dad was away for almost two months on his last trip.

MY SCORE

Day 4

1. Underline the proper adjective.
   Last week, I received a postcard from my friend who is Japanese.
2. Is the underlined word a proper adjective?
   Yes ☐ No ☐
   She had sent me some Asian sweets she had bought in Korea.
3. Correct the spelling mistake. ______________
   It's important to indickate with hand signals when riding a bike.
4. A synonym for ***synthetic*** is ______________.
   natural artificial expensive
5. Write the homophone for ***clause***. ______________
6. Number the words in alphabetical order.
   money ____ month ____ monster ____ monk ____
7. Add a prefix to make the words mean ***not***.
   ____happy ____able ____like
8. ***she had*** or ***she would***?
   I know that ______________ been wanting a new bike for a while.
9. Punctuate the sentence.
   the tour de france is an annual cycling race which has been held since 1903
10. Add speech marks to show what was said.
    Watch out! the cyclist yelled as he sped past. You're in the way!
11. Add apostrophes for contraction or possession.
    The bikes front tyre clipped anothers rear tyre and caused an accident.
12. Circle the nouns.
    The cyclists, who come from all over the world, ride in teams.
13. Circle the idiom (common expression).
    The cyclist from the Spanish team had a short fuse.
14. Rewrite in the simple future tense.
    I trained for the race. ______________
15. Question ☐, exclamation ☐ or statement ☐?
    There have been many doping scandals surrounding the race over the years ☐

MY SCORE

Day 5

1. Circle the proper adjective.
   The guide, who was Italian, shared lots of interesting facts with our tour group.
2. The underlined word is a proper adjective ☐ or proper noun ☐?
   The Italian guide had run tours all throughout Europe.
3. Unjumble the jumbled word. ______________
   Our dog is very arsevigesg towards cats.
4. The antonym for ***wonderful*** is ______________.
   amazing impressive ordinary
5. ***clause*** or ***claws***?
   There was a secret ______________ in the contract.
6. The underlined word comes first in alphabetical order. Yes ☐ No ☐
   represent repeat replay repent report
7. Add the suffix ***en*** to these adjectives.
   moist____ loose____ wide____
8. Write the missing word. ***colony*** ***plague***
   A ______________ of ants.
9. Punctuate the sentence.
   whats the most interesting case youve ever worked on
10. Add a comma.
    When collecting evidence detectives must ensure they don't contaminate the crime scene.
11. Add one or more apostrophes.
    If there arent any fingerprints to collect, a detectives job is to find other clues.
12. Circle the nouns.
    The witness gave a statement to the detective.
13. Write ***it's*** or ***its***.
    The detective's tracking dog wagged ______________ tail and followed the scent.
14. Rewrite in the simple past tense.
    The detective will catch the criminal.
    ____
15. Which adverb—***dejectedly*** or ***hopefully***?
    The detective explained ______________ that there were absolutely no leads.

MY SCORE

Skill focus

Masculine and feminine nouns

Nouns are important words. They are used to name people, places, things, feelings or ideas.

Masculine nouns are the names given to male people or animals.

Feminine nouns are the names given to female people and animals. Often, the suffix ***ess*** is added to the end of words to change them into feminine nouns.

	People	Animals
Masculine	father son man husband	stallion gander boar lion
Feminine	mother daughter woman wife	mare goose sow lioness

These types of nouns are called **gender nouns**. Not all nouns have a gender. Many nouns like person, parents and children have no gender at all.

Practice questions

1. Underline the masculine noun in blue and the feminine noun in orange.
   - (a) *The hero and heroine in the film held hands and jumped from building to building.*
   - (b) *After the wedding, the newly married husband and wife travelled to France for their honeymoon.*
   - (c) *The lion fiercely guarded the lioness and her cubs from the hunters.*

Day 1

1. Underline the masculine noun.

   The lady's husband was not injured in the accident.

2. The underlined word is a feminine noun ☐ or a collective noun ☐?

   Medics and firefighters assisted the injured <u>woman</u>.

3. Unjumble the jumbled word. ______________

   I can't ptcace your invitation as I'm busy.

4. Another word for anxious is:

   happy   worried   thirsty

5. Write ***breathe*** and ***breath*** in the correct places.

   Take a deep ______________ in then ______________ out through your nose.

6. Expand the contraction in context. ______________

   It's going to be raining all weekend!

7. Circle two words that can be built from ***show***.

   shower   unshow   showman   showroom

8. ***clutch*** or ***swarm***?

   A ______________ of bees.

9. Punctuate the sentence.

   invitations are given out for events such as parties weddings and christenings

10. Add commas to enclose the additional information.

    An RSVP originally a French phrase is given to the host so they know who will be attending.

11. Circle the conjunction.

    You should RSVP by the requested date so the host can be prepared for the event.

12. Circle the verb groups.

    We were looking for a present but my brother was annoying me.

13. Circle the adverbial of frequency.

    George has a huge birthday party every year—it's always a great event!

14. Circle the pronouns.

    My sister and I wrapped all of the presents neatly and we were proud of ourselves.

15. Circle the prepositions.

    The guests went into the garden and played games beneath the oak tree.

Day 2

1. Underline the feminine noun.

   The cow and her calf were kept in a separate pen.

2. The underlined word is a masculine noun ☐ or a collective noun ☐?

   Bulls leave the herd but cows stay all their lives.

3. Rearrange the letters to make a word that means ***10 × 8***. teihgy ____________

4. Another word for ***combine*** is:

   separate juggle join

5. ***for*** or ***four***?

   It takes me ____________ minutes to make a cup of tea myself.

6. The underlined word comes first in alphabetical order. Yes ☐ No ☐

   psycho psalm psoriasis psychic

7. What is the base word of ***methodology*** and ***methodical***? ____________

8. ***dye*** or ***die***?

   Will our plants ____________ if we put coloured ____________ in their water?

9. Are speech marks needed? Yes ☐ No ☐

   Mr Smith said he was pleased with our work.

10. Add a comma to clarify meaning.

    While Mr Smith was talking a knock on the door interrupted the class.

11. Circle the nouns.

    Before a big test, you should drink water, do all your homework and get plenty of sleep.

12. Write the word that shows a stronger obligation.

    must ***could***

    You ____________ study for each exam.

13. Circle the error.

    Its not about luck, but about staying calm and having belief in your ability.

14. Circle the word used to tell who the underlined noun belongs to.

    Our school achieved some of the highest exam results in the country!

15. Circle the conjunction.

    I'm relieved that our tests are over, but I'm also sad to be finishing school forever.

MY SCORE

Day 3

1. Underline the masculine noun.

   Some diseases more commonly affect males than females.

2. The underlined word is a feminine noun ☐ or a collective noun ☐?

   Heart disease is common on my mother's side of the family.

3. Correct the spelling mistake. ____________

   The restaurant revew in the magazine was interesting.

4. The underlined word is the synonym ☐ or antonym ☐ for ***calm***?

   peaceful turbulent choppy

5. Write the homophone for ***bawl***. ____________

6. Expand the contraction in context. ____________

   When's the critic expected to arrive?

7. Circle three words that can be built from ***do***.

   doable down did dome doesn't

8. ***kangaroos*** or ***wolves***?

   A pack of ____________.

9. Are speech marks needed? Yes ☐ No ☐

   Do you know which country haggis, kilts, bagpipes and the Loch Ness monster come from? asked Uncle Joe.

10. Add speech marks to show what was said.

    I think they all come from Scotland, am I right? I answered uncertainly.

11. Underline the nouns.

    The tourist took many photographs of the beautiful landscape.

12. Circle the verb group.

    This bus must have been travelling for many hours.

13. Add a preposition.

    The group crossed ____________ an old bridge and listened to the water rushing below.

14. Circle the adjectives.

    The rocky hills were covered in lush, green grass.

15. ***because*** or ***although***?

    I'd like to visit Scotland, ____________ I am interested in its history.

MY SCORE

WEEK 27

WEEK 27

Day 4

1. Underline the feminine noun.

   The hen scavenged around the vegetable garden.

2. The underlined word is a masculine noun ☐ or collective noun ☐?

   The <u>rooster</u> and hen had a clutch of eggs.

3. Correct the spelling mistake. ______________

   The semetary in the small town had some very old gravestones in it.

4. The antonym for ***wealth*** is ______________.

   success kindness poverty

5. ***rose*** or ***rows***?

   I picked a red ______________ from the garden.

6. Which word comes directly before ***prince*** in alphabetical order?

   prune present practical predict

7. What is the base word of ***inflated*** and ***inflatable***? ______________

8. ***wheel*** or ***we'll***?

   I think ______________ need to replace that old bicycle ______________, as it's rusty.

9. Punctuate the sentence.

   mosquitoes are arguably the most dangerous insects because of the diseases they transmit

10. Is the black comma correct? Yes ☐ No ☐

    Malaria is a disease carried by mosquitoes in tropical Africa, Asia, and South America.

11. Circle the conjunction.

    A mosquito's life cycle has four stages, and most species lay their eggs near water.

12. Write the missing verb in its correct form. ***have***

    Have you ______________ your travel vaccinations?

13. Circle the word used to tell who the underlined noun belongs to.

    I have done my <u>research</u> and I'm prepared.

14. Write the missing pronoun.

    Mosquitoes pierce the animal's skin with a proboscis and then ______________ drink its blood.

15. Question ☐, statement ☐ or command ☐?

    Not all species of mosquito feed on blood ☐

MY SCORE

Day 5

1. Underline the masculine noun.

   My dad is teaching me how to play golf.

2. The underlined word is a feminine noun ☐ or collective noun ☐?

   The little girl eagerly helped her dad carry his <u>set of golf clubs</u>.

3. Correct the spelling mistake. ______________

   A profeshional dancer came to our school to give us lessons.

4. The antonym for ***abbreviate*** is ______________.

   shorten lengthen cut enough

5. Write the homophone for ***stationary***. ______________

6. Expand the contraction in context. ______________

   Do you know what's being built around the corner?

7. Circle two words that can be built from ***deceive***.

   deceptive deception decision decisive

8. ***coven*** or ***flock***?

   A ______________ of witches.

9. Punctuate the sentence.

   latin ballroom ballet and breakdancing are different styles of dance

10. Add speech marks to show what was said.

    The dancer asked the children, Would you like to learn the steps of this dance?

11. Circle the conjunction.

    The dancer twirled her sparkling skirt as she glided gracefully around the room.

12. Write the missing verb in its correct form. ***step***

    One of the boys kept ______________ on his poor partner's feet.

13. Circle the word used to tell who the underlined noun belongs to.

    We saw the dancers compete on our <u>television</u>.

14. Circle the pronoun and the noun(s) it refers to.

    When she was on the stage, the ballet dancer performed brilliantly.

15. Question ☐, command ☐ or statement ☐?

    Many cultures have their own traditional dances ☐

MY SCORE

Negative form

Verb groups are verbs that have two parts—one or more helping verbs and a main verb.

In some verb groups, the helping verb changes the meaning of the main verb.

Some of these helping verbs are:

can *will* *might* *may*

could *should* *would*

For example: *You* ***will*** ***go*** *swimming after school.*

The meaning of the sentence can be made opposite by adding the word 'not' to the end of these helping verbs. This changes the sentence to a **negative form**.

For example: *You* ***will*** ***not*** ***go*** *swimming after school.*

To make a sentence without a verb group negative, add a helping verb like *do*, *be* or *have* in its correct form, and the word *not*. For example:

I like to eat eggs for breakfast.

I do not like to eat eggs for breakfast.

To make your sentence easier to read, the helping verb and word ***not*** can be made into a contraction (will not ⟶ won't).

Practice questions

1. Rewrite in the negative form.
   He gives her flowers.
   ____
2. Circle the negative verb form and write as a contraction.
   She will not be happy.
   ____

Day 1

1. Rewrite in the negative form.
   I travel very often. ____________
2. Circle the negative verb group and write as a contraction.
   I would not like to travel to Spain. ____________
3. Unjumble the jumbled word. ____________
   The young children htgouf over the popular toy.
4. The antonym for ***adequate*** is ____________.
   opposite enough insufficient ample
5. Add the suffix ***able*** to these words.
   believe____ laugh____ admire____
6. Expand the contraction in context. ____________
   'You'd better not have muddy shoes!' Mum said.
7. ***aloud*** or ***allowed***?
   He read the poem ____________.
8. Circle the correct idiom.
   over the moon over the sun
9. Punctuate the sentence.
   the worlds oceans cover over 70% of the planet and the pacific ocean is the largest
10. Add one or more commas.
    Cape Agulhas South Africa is the place where the Atlantic and Indian Oceans meet.
11. Add one or more apostrophes.
    In some places, the waters dont mix due to differences in their density.
12. The underlined words are: comparative ☐ or superlative adjectives ☐?
    The Arctic Ocean, the world's smallest and shallowest, is mostly frozen during the winter.
13. Write the comparative or superlative form of ***warm***.
    Fortunately, the weather was ____________ during our holiday than it usually is at home.
14. Rewrite in the simple present tense.
    We looked out over the horizon.
    ____
15. Which adverb better expresses the meaning?
    excitedly ***furiously***
    The boy screamed ____________ during his tantrum.

MY SCORE

Day 2

1. Rewrite in the negative form.

   She likes her job. ______________________

2. Circle the negative verb group and write as a contraction. ______________

   She will not get all her work done quickly.

3. Correct the spelling mistake. ______________

   The broken mashine needs to be repaired.

4. A synonym for ***ambitious*** is ______________.

   lazy   driven   indifferent

5. Add prefixes to make the words mean the opposite.

   ____behave   ____tangle

6. Expand the contraction in context. ______________

   Who's got the time please?

7. Write the homophone for ***patients***. ______________

8. ***then*** or ***than***?

   We'll visit Sarah and ______________ David because her house is closer ______________ his to here.

9. Punctuate the sentence.

   gina frosts secretary was always very busy scheduling her appointments

10. Circle the sentence type.   direct   reported

    The visitor announced he had an appointment with Mrs Frost.

11. Add speech marks to show what was said.

    Your next client is here, Mrs Frost, she announced over the intercom.

12. Circle the masculine noun.

    The receptionist took down the gentleman's details to enter into the database.

13. ***there*** or ***they're***?

    'Please wait over ______________', she instructed.

14. Circle the pronouns and the noun they refer to.

    When the next client arrived she was offered coffee to drink while she waited.

15. Question ☐, command ☐ or statement ☐?

    When will my next client be arriving ☐

MY SCORE

Day 3

1. Rewrite in the negative form.

   I enjoy science classes. ______________________

2. Circle the negative verb group and write as a contraction. ______________

   I cannot wait for our next lesson.

3. Correct the spelling mistake. ______________

   As you get older, your eyesite generally deteriorates.

4. The underlined word is a synonym ☐ or antonym ☐ for ***aid***?

   assist   <u>hinder</u>   help   destroy

5. Add the suffix ***ion*** to these verbs.

   elect____   decide____   explode____

6. Expand the contraction in context. ______________

   It's been raining heavily for a whole week!

7. Write the homophone for ***pane***. ______________

8. Circle the correct idiom.

   To bury the carving knife   *To bury the hatchet*

9. Punctuate the sentence.

   fred hollows was a well known ophthalmologist who came from new zealand

10. Add commas.

    The Fred Hollows Foundation established in 1992 helps to restore sight to people across Australia Asia and Africa.

11. Add one or more apostrophes.

    Charities work to improve peoples health and education.

12. Write the comparative or superlative form of ***bad***.

    Aid is provided to areas that are ______________ affected by poverty, war and natural disasters.

13. Circle the adverbs.

    The aid worker worked tirelessly but rested briefly to help the people.

14. Circle the pronouns and the noun they refer to.

    Mary felt good about herself when she donated some money.

15. Is the word ***resolution*** used correctly?

    Yes ☐   No ☐

    I have made a resolution to work for a volunteer organisation one day a week this year.

MY SCORE

Day 4

1. Rewrite in the negative form.
   I like to read. ______________
2. Circle the negative verb group and write as a contraction. ______________
   You should not watch too much television.
3. Correct the spelling mistake. ______________
   We needed to seperate the two dogs, as they kept fighting.
4. The synonym for ***complex*** is ______________.
   simple complicated combined
5. Add prefixes to make the words mean the opposite.
   ____known ____even
6. Expand the contraction in context. ______________
   Dad's been learning Japanese for two years now.
7. Write the homophone for ***where***. ______________
8. ***Sum*** or ***Some***?
   ______________ *mathematical calculations are more difficult than others.*
9. Punctuate the sentence.
   famous novelists from english speaking countries include charles dickens mark twain and miles franklin
10. Circle the sentence type. direct reported
    I asked Mum what her favourite book was and she said it was Jane Eyre.
11. Add speech marks to show what was said.
    What's your favourite novel? she asked me in return.
12. Circle the feminine noun.
    The writer's wife was the illustrator of his stories.
13. ***foreword*** or ***forward***?
    The book's ______________ *acknowledged the author's family and friends.*
14. Write the missing verb in its correct form. ***write***
    The prolific writer has ______________ *hundreds of novels.*
15. Exclamation ☐, statement ☐ or question ☐?
    This novel is funny, entertaining and sometimes sad☐

MY SCORE

Day 5

1. Rewrite in the negative form.
   Gordon speaks Mandarin. ______________
2. Circle the negative verb group and write as a contraction. ______________
   Gordon's brother did not learn Mandarin.
3. Rearrange the letters to make a word that means ***the taste of something***.
   vruofal ______________
4. The antonym for ***condense*** is ______________.
   compress enrage expand
5. Add the suffix ***ion*** to these verbs.
   collide____ collect____
6. Expand the contraction in context. ______________
   Sarah's been to Thailand, India and China before.
7. Write the homophone for ***sew***. ______________
8. Circle the correct idiom.
   A tea bag in a teacup *A storm in a teacup*
9. Punctuate the sentence.
   china and india are two of the world's most populous countries and they are located on the asian continent
10. Add commas.
    Karachi Pakistan and Mumbai India are two cities with over 12 million inhabitants.
11. Add one or more apostrophes.
    Indonesias island of Java is the worlds most populous island with over 130 million inhabitants.
12. Underline the noun phrases.
    The Philippines has a population nearing 100 million people.
13. Circle the proper adjective.
    The Chinese government decided to develop population control measures in 1979.
14. Circle the proper nouns.
    It is predicted that India, which doesn't have such measures in place, will eventually overtake China as the world's most populous country.
15. Which adjective fits better? ***quietest*** ***busiest***
    Singapore has one of the world's ______________ *ports with thousands of ships passing through it.*

MY SCORE

Skill focus

Demonstrative determiners

The words ***this***, ***these***, ***that*** and ***those*** are used before a noun.

They tell us whether the thing or person is near or far away.

Use **this** with singular nouns near you.

This *cake is delicious.*

Use **these** with plural nouns near you.

These *biscuits are tasty.*

Use **that** with singular nouns far from you.

*Is **that** boy your brother?*

Use **those** with plural nouns far from you.

Those *boys are by the swings.*

Practice questions

1. Which would be closer?

   these chairs those chairs

2. ***this*** or ***these?***

   Have you seen __________ new book?

Day 1

1. Which would be closer?

   this pencil that pencil

2. ***this*** or ***these***?

   Can you please take __________ pencil?

3. Correct the spelling mistake. __________

   The explanashion you gave for being late won't do.

4. The synonym for ***feeble*** is __________.

   strong weak productive

5. Write the homophone for ***raise***. __________

6. Which word comes directly before ***muscle*** in the dictionary?

   murder murmur muse mural

7. Add prefixes to make the words mean ***among*** and ***under***.

   ____national ____marine

8. Complete the simile. ***daisy*** or ***pear***?

   As fresh as a __________.

9. Punctuate the sentence.

   toys are important for childrens development and are found across all countries and cultures around the world

10. Add commas to enclose the additional information.

    Electronic toys although becoming increasingly popular haven't replaced traditional toys entirely.

11. Add ***which*** or ***who***.

    The popular toy Barbie™, __________ has been produced since 1959, was created by Ruth Handler.

12. Circle the proper adjective.

    Lego™, a Danish invention, has been a popular toy for over 50 years.

13. ***ensure*** or ***insure***?

    If you are travelling you should __________ that you __________ your belongings in case they are lost or stolen.

14. Which tense? ***past*** ***present*** ***future***

    The toy fair is being held next year in January.

15. Circle the negative verb form and write as a contraction. __________

    The children are not good at packing away their toys.

Day 2

1. Add the correct words. ***that*** ***those***

   ________ paper ________ papers

2. ***that*** or ***those***?

   Where are ________ papers I left on the table?

3. Rearrange ***Inacubmae*** to make a word that means a vehicle for transporting patients.

   ____

4. The root ***phon*** in ***telephone*** and ***phonics*** means:

   sound picture earth

5. ***sow*** or ***sew***?

   The farmer had to ________ the button onto his shirt.

6. Which word comes directly after ***sinister*** in the dictionary?

   singular sinus single sister

7. Circle two words that can be built from ***watch***.

   watchmaker offwatch wristwatch watchs

8. Complete the simile.

   As bold as br ________.

9. Punctuate the sentence.

   the new editor for the evening chronicle will be announced on monday

10. Add one or more apostrophes.

    The journalists teamwork was rewarded when their article appeared on the papers front page.

11. Underline the noun phrases.

    The long and boring article covered the whole page and had no photographs.

12. Underline the verb groups.

    The writer has been working on her article for many hours so she should take a well-earned break.

13. ***right*** and ***write***.

    You must get all your facts ________ when you ________ for a newspaper.

14. Which tense? ***past*** ***present*** ***future***

    Jan is always reading as many articles as she can.

15. Add ***who*** or ***whose***.

    One journalist, ________ career had taken her to many war-torn regions, was awarded for her work.

MY SCORE

Day 3

1. Which would be far away?

   these chairs those chairs

2. ***this*** or ***that***?

   Can you please bring me ________ chair over there?

3. Correct the spelling mistake. ________

   Some ancient societies would sacrifice anamils for the gods.

4. The antonym for ***feasible*** is ________.

   doable impossible practical

5. Write the homophone for ***pause***. ________

6. Circle the negative verb group and write as a contraction. ________

   My brother will not finish his homework.

7. Add the prefix ***anti*** meaning ***corrective***.

   ____histamine ____biotic ____septic

8. Complete the simile. ***pet*** or ***post***?

   As deaf as a ________.

9. Punctuate the sentence.

   there are many thousands of species of butterflies and moths including the monarch butterfly and luna moth

10. Add one or more apostrophes.

    A butterflys diet typically consists of liquids, including nectar from flowers and juices from rotting fruits.

11. ***whose*** or ***that***?

    The butterfly ________ fluttered into the room looked as light as a feather.

12. Write the missing verb in its correct form. ***fly***

    The butterfly had ________ from the flower to my finger.

13. ***to*** or ***too***?

    It then flew ________ a nearby tree branch.

14. Which tense? ***past*** ***present*** ***future***

    The photographer is a keen butterfly enthusiast.

15. Circle the preposition.

    When I visited the zoo, I saw many beautiful butterflies in the butterfly house.

MY SCORE

WEEK 29

Day 4

1. Add the correct words. ***this*** ***these***

   _________ toy _________ toys

2. ***This*** or ***Those***?

   _________ toys are inside the toy box.

3. Correct the spelling mistake. _________

   It is important to get a good educashun.

4. The part of the words that means ***life*** is _________.

   biography biology biochemistry

5. Write ***would*** and ***wood*** in the correct places.

   I _________ chop some _________ but I've hurt my hand.

6. Circle the negative verb group and write as a contraction. _________

   Joanne has not slept soundly this week.

7. Circle two words that can be built from ***recognise***.

   recognition recogniser

   recognisement recognisable

8. Complete the simile.

   As white as s_________.

9. Punctuate the sentence.

   the bazaar district in cairo egypt is a major attraction for tourists and locals

10. Add commas to the description.

    The wide-eyed curious tourists were surprised to see so many colourful shiny and interesting items for sale.

11. Circle two feminine nouns.

    Mum was looking for many hours for the perfect gift for Granny.

12. The underlined words are: verb groups/ noun phrases

    We purchased a decorative tea set and some mint tea.

13. ***through*** or ***threw***?

    Mum accidentally _________ out my ticket so I had to look _________ the rubbish for it.

14. Which tense? ***past*** ***present*** ***future***

    We won't be returning home until next week.

15. Circle the nouns.

    This holiday has been my favourite so far—the pyramids were amazing.

MY SCORE

Day 5

1. Which would be closer?

   that house this house

2. ***that*** or ***those***?

   Is _________ house yours?

3. Correct the spelling mistake. _________

   The brave young boy didn't hesetate before jumping into the freezing water.

4. A synonym for ***hospitable*** is _________.

   surgery welcoming unfriendly

5. Write the homophone for ***led***. _________

6. Circle the negative verb group and write as a contraction. _________

   The race should not start for another hour.

7. Add prefixes to make the words mean the opposite.

   ____pronounce ____perfect

8. Complete the simile. ***tree*** or ***bell***?

   As clear as a _________.

9. Punctuate the sentence.

   oyster farms have been operating on frances atlantic coast for centuries

10. Add one or more apostrophes.

    Oysters are farmed for pearls and for their meat. An oysters life can span up to 20 years.

11. ***whose*** or ***that***?

    I found an oyster _________ shell contained a beautiful pearl.

12. Write the missing verb in its correct form. ***grow***

    The oysters in the farm _________ rapidly.

13. ***pare*** or ***pear*** or ***pair***?

    Dad needs to buy a new _________ of shoes.

14. Which tense? ***past*** ***present*** ***future***

    Oysters can produce more than one pearl at a time.

15. Is the word ***form*** used correctly? Yes ☐ No ☐

    Pearls, which can take from months to years to fully form, are popular additions to jewellery items.

How do suffixes change words?

Suffixes are letters joined to the end of words to make new words. They can also change how words are used in a sentence. Look at some of these examples:

clever (adjective)	clever + ly	cleverly (adverb)
teach (verb)	teach + er	teacher (noun)
poison (noun)	poison + ous	poisonous (adjective)
enjoy (verb)	enjoy + able	enjoyable (adjective)
soft (adjective)	soft + en	soften (verb)
happy (adjective)	happy + ness	happiness (noun)

Knowing how a suffix changes the meaning of a word is important. It helps make your writing clearer and allows you to explain things in many different ways.

Practice questions

1. The suffix ***ly*** changes the adj____________ to an adv____________.
   clever____ polite____ wise____
2. The suffix ***er*** changes the v____________ to a n____________.
   garden____ paint____ sing____

1. Add the suffix ***ion*** to change the verbs to nouns.
   discuss____ admit____
2. The suffix ***ness*** changes the words from adj____________ to n____________.
   polite____ clever____ swift____
3. Rearrange the letters to make a word that means a ***large rock***.
   lebodur ____________
4. Circle an antonym for ***humiliate***.
   embarrass honour discuss
5. Number the words in alphabetical order.
   numeracy ____ numb ____
   number ____ numerical ____
6. Write the homophone for ***hear***. ____________
7. Circle the idiom (common expression).
   We missed our flight home, but we hit the jackpot as they upgraded us to first class.
8. Punctuate the sentence.
   gold mining ghost towns can be found in remote areas of some countries
9. Add commas.
   Many major gold rushes took place across parts of Australia Brazil Canada South Africa and the United States of America in the 1800s.
10. Add one or more apostrophes.
    Thousands moved to try to make their fortunes, but many didnt find what they were looking for.
11. Underline the noun phrases.
    The hard-working miner sat heavily on the creaky old stool and enjoyed his icy-cold drink.
12. Write ***under*** or ***over***.
    When it was too hot, the miners sought shelter ____________ the spindly trees.
13. ***Its*** or ***It's***?
    ____________ *difficult work looking for gold!*
14. Circle the conjunction.
    Most of the miners found nothing and lost all of their money trying to find the precious metal.
15. Add the correct question word.
    ____________ *did the gold rushes end?*

MY SCORE

WEEK 30

Day 2

1. Add the suffix ***ant*** to change the verbs to adjectives.

   hesitate____ tolerate____

2. The suffix ***ly*** changes the adj__________ to adv__________.

   bright____ proud____ nervous____

3. Correct the spelling mistake. __________

   The graysful ballet dancers glided across the room.

4. An antonym for ***generous*** is __________.

   kind selfish unhappy welcoming

5. Expand the contraction in context. __________

   Dad said he'd like some help in the garden.

6. ***whether*** or ***weather***?

   Do you know __________ *the* __________ *will be nice for your holiday?*

7. One man. Two __________.

8. Punctuate the sentence.

   birds such as swans peacocks and seagulls were once served at banquets

9. Add commas to enclose the additional information.

   Queen Victoria who reigned over Britain for almost 64 years became queen at the age of 18.

10. Add an apostrophe for contraction or possession.

    Victoria wasnt the first Queen of England.

11. How many pronouns? __________

    The Queen carefully hid her jewels whenever she went away from the palace.

12. Circle the preposition.

    The largest and most spectacular palace is in Madrid.

13. Underline the adverbial of frequency.

    Every winter, the royal family move to their winter palace.

14. Circle the conjunction.

    Because of a security risk, the royal family had to stay in their palace.

15. Circle the masculine noun.

    Hesitantly, the small prince peeked out of the window and was told sternly to move away.

MY SCORE

Day 3

1. Add the suffix ***ence*** to change the adjectives to nouns.

   confident____ obedient____

2. The suffix ***ant*** changes the v__________ to adj__________.

   tolerate____ observe____

3. Correct the spelling mistake. __________

   The junior lawyer wanted to become a partnar.

4. The underlined word is the synonym ☐ or antonym ☐ for ***gather***?

   scatter <u>collect</u> grow

5. Number the words in alphabetical order.

   exercise ____ exceptional ____ examination ____

6. Write the homophone for ***heir***. __________

7. Circle the idiom (common expression).

   After he was arrested, the criminal said he was turning over a new leaf and would never break the law again.

8. Punctuate the sentence.

   luxury yachts are commonly seen docked in ports along the mediterranean coast

9. Add commas.

   The cities of Cannes France and Split Croatia are popular places to visit.

10. How many apostrophes are needed? __________

    The Mediterranean islands beautiful beaches are popular tourist attractions.

11. Is the underlined word a verb ☐ or an adjective ☐?

    One <u>interesting</u> attraction in the region is the active volcano, Mt Etna.

12. Underline the adverbial of time.

    In 79 BCE, the eruption of Mount Vesuvius led to the destruction of Pompeii.

13. The underlined words are: verbs adjectives

    The <u>learned</u> guide had a wealth of <u>interesting</u> information to share with the group.

14. Circle the conjunction.

    Although the tour was interesting, there was a lot of information to take in!

15. Circle the adverbs.

    One beautiful day recently, we hiked leisurely up the mountain.

MY SCORE

Day 4

1. Add the suffix ***er*** to change these verbs to nouns.

   juggle____ paint____ design____

2. The suffix ***ise*** changes the n____________

   to v____________.

   terror____ vapour____ colony____

3. Correct the spelling mistake. ____________

   It is nesesary to peel an orange before you can eat it.

4. A synonym for ***monotonous*** is ____________.

   similar boring interesting

5. Expand the contraction in context. ____________

   My little sisters going to school next year.

6. ***dual*** or ***duel***?

   Is the road a ____________ carriageway?

7. One foot. Two ____________.

8. Punctuate the sentence.

   two species which are endangered are the yangtze and the amazon river dolphins

9. Add commas.

   Several species such as the snow leopard the tiger the giant panda and the blue whale are endangered.

10. Add an apostrophe for contraction or possession.

    A dolphins blowhole is used to draw breath and also expel air.

11. Write the missing pronoun.

    A dolphin that becomes separated from its pod must fend for ____________.

12. Circle the preposition.

    The dolphins were frolicking playfully in the water.

13. ***wasn't*** or ***weren't***?

    One dolphin ____________ shy, coming very close to the swimmers.

14. Circle the conjunction.

    Since dolphins are highly intelligent, they have been trained and used as search and rescue animals.

15. ***That*** or ***Those***?

    ____________ dolphins eat mainly fish and squid.

MY SCORE

Day 5

WEEK 30

1. Add the suffix ***ly*** to change the adjectives to adverbs.

   bright____ proud____ nervous____

2. The suffix ***able*** changes the v____________

   to adj____________.

   respect____ notice____ move____

3. Unjumble the jumbled word. ____________

   I won't be balaviael to meet with you until next week.

4. The antonym for ***scrawny*** is ____________.

   skinny chubby gaunt

5. The underlined word comes first in alphabetical order. Yes ☐ No ☐

   prognosis pregnancy <u>present</u> prairie

6. Write the homophone for ***plain***. ____________

7. Circle the idiom (common expression).

   The boy was so excited for his holiday; he was acting like he had a bee in his bonnet.

8. Punctuate the sentence.

   oranges are grown in brazil plums are grown in china and pineapples in the philippines

9. Add commas to enclose the additional information.

   Tomatoes commonly referred to as vegetables are correctly classified as a fruit.

10. Add one or more apostrophes.

    A strawberrys seeds are on the outside of the fruit and a tomatos seeds are on the inside.

11. Is the underlined word a verb ☐ or an adjective ☐?

    The fruit was <u>growing</u> quickly and would soon be ready for harvest.

12. Is the underlined word a verb ☐ or an adjective ☐?

    The <u>growing</u> boy was encouraged to eat fruit.

13. ***was*** or ***were***?

    When it ____________ time for dessert the children ____________ happy to be served fresh fruit salad.

14. Which adverb—***keenly*** or ***lazily***?

    The interested children ____________ tended to their school's vegetable garden.

15. ***That*** or ***This***?

    ____________ plum tree over there has dropped fruit all over the ground.

MY SCORE

Skill focus

Plural nouns from other languages

English borrows many words from other languages such as Latin, French and Greek.

Often this means that there are different rules for making them plural.

Let's explore two of these irregular plurals below.

Words ending with *us*

One cactus

Two cacti

One hippopotamus

Two hippopotami

When words end with ***us*** a plural can be made by changing ***us*** to ***i***.

Words ending with *is*

One crisis

Two crises

One oasis

Two oases

When words end with ***is*** a plural can be made by changing ***is*** to ***es***.

Practice questions

1. Circle the plural of ***oasis***.

   oasis   oases

2. Write the singular of ***hippopotami***.

   ____

Day 1

1. Circle the plural of ***oasis***.   oasises   oases
2. Write the singular of of ***cacti***. ______________
3. Correct the spelling mistake. ______________

   You must evacuate the building imediatly in case of fire.

4. Write the homophone for ***piece***. ______________
5. The underlined word is the synonym ☐ or antonym ☐ for ***serene***?

   <u>peaceful</u>   disturbed   hysterical

6. Expand the contraction in context. ______________

   He's been caught in the rain so many times!

7. Adding the suffix ***er*** changes these

   v______________ to n______________.

   manage____   gamble____   speak____

8. Punctuate the sentence.

   the adventure camp was visited by the school children each may

9. Circle the word that tells who the underlined noun belongs to.

   Can you help me unpack when you have finished making your <u>bed</u>?

10. Circle the word that does not belong.

    I was looking forward to abseiling and kayaking river, as I had never tried either before.

11. Circle the verb groups.

    The instructor couldn't praise the children's teamwork enough, and he believed they should all be rewarded on their return to school.

12. Circle the adverbial of time.

    On Thursday evening there was a special dinner and a disco.

13. Add ***that*** or ***those***.

    The activity ______________ *was the scariest was the flying fox.*

14. Circle the adverbs.

    Some children were incredibly frightened of heights and nervously approached the edge.

15. Circle the prepositions.

    The children ran across the field and climbed over the gate.

Day 2

1. Circle the plural of ***octopus***.

   octopuses   octopi

2. Write the singular of ***oases***. ______________

3. Rearrange the letters to make a word that means a ***leafy salad vegetable***.

   cetulte ______________

4. ***pane*** or ***pain***?

   The ______________ of glass didn't break.

5. Write ***principal*** or ***principle*** in the correct place.

   The ______________ aim of the camp was team building.

6. Which word comes directly before ***stone*** in alphabetical order?

   stair   steep   stay   still   stuck

7. Add the prefix ***extra*** to these words.

   ____ordinary   ____curricular

8. Are speech marks needed? Yes ☐ No ☐

   Nutrition experts recommend that we eat five servings of vegetables each day.

9. Add commas to clarify meaning.

   Eating vegetables we were told can protect against a number of diseases.

10. Circle the nouns.

    Drinking water regularly, as well as receiving regular (safe) exposure to sunlight, also keeps people healthy.

11. Circle the verb groups.

    You should eat all your vegetables or you will not be healthy.

12. Write the comparative or superlative form of ***easy***.

    One of the ______________ meals to prepare is a salad.

13. Write ***those*** or ***these***.

    I need ______________ vegetables for my recipe: five potatoes, a parsnip, some beans, two onions and a few carrots.

14. Circle the pronouns.

    After they ate, the children cleaned up after themselves.

15. Circle the preposition.

    The cabbage in the pot was boiling.

MY SCORE

Day 3

WEEK 31

1. Circle the plural of ***diagnosis***.

   diagnosises   diagnoses

2. Write the singular of ***octopi***. ______________

3. Correct the spelling mistake. ______________

   I like to browse through toy sale katalogues.

4. Write the homophone for ***meddle***. ______________

5. The antonym for ***turmoil*** is ______________.

   tranquility   commotion   disturbance

6. Expand the contraction in context. ______________

   Where's the cat food? In the cupboard?

7. Adding the suffix ***ant*** changes these

   v______________ to adj______________.

   observe____   tolerate____   expect____

8. Punctuate the sentence.

   stilt fishermen who fish off sri lankas south coast sit or stand on wooden poles

9. Add speech marks to show what was said.

   Wow! He's caught a big one! the observer exclaimed.

10. Circle the conjunction.

    Sustainable fishing practices are important so that fish stocks are not completely depleted.

11. Circle the verb group.

    The fisherman had been catching fish from the old boat for many years.

12. Circle the adjectives.

    The smelly, rickety old boat was destroyed in the severe storm.

13. ***because*** or ***although***?

    I like to eat fish, ______________ I don't like to catch them!

14. The underlined word is a pronoun.
    Yes ☐ No ☐

    Which is the best tasting <u>fish</u>?

15. Add a preposition.

    The fish was too big for the child to reel ______________ alone.

Day 4

1. Circle the plural of ***cactus***. cacti cactuses
2. Write the singular of ***diagnoses***. ______________
3. Correct the spelling mistake. ______________
   Place each animal card into a kategory it can belong to.
4. ***sea*** or ***see***?
   Can you ____________ the ____________ from there?
5. ***profit*** or ***prophet***?
   The company has announced its largest
   ______________ to date.
6. The underlined word comes first in alphabetical order. Yes ☐ No ☐
   <u>greenery</u> grocery greatest
7. Add a prefix meaning ***out of***. ____port ____hale
8. Are speech marks needed?
   Have you ever been diving in the Red Sea? asked the diving instructor.
9. Add commas.
   The Red Sea which separates Asia and Africa is a popular sea with divers.
10. Circle the proper adjective.
    Hurghada is a popular Egyptian resort town near the Red Sea.
11. Write the missing verb in its correct form. ***live***
    The Red Sea has many species of fish
    ______________ in it.
12. Circle the superlative adjectives.
    The sea has some of the brightest and most beautiful fish, corals and sea creatures.
13. Add ***that*** or ***those***.
    The Red Sea has a shoreline ______________ borders many countries.
14. Write the missing pronouns.
    In a Bible story, Moses was responsible for leading his people out of Egypt. ______________ parted the Red Sea for all of ______________ to cross.
15. Write ***choose*** or ***chose***.
    Visitors to the town who come to enjoy the warm weather and the sea have many hotels to ______________ from.

MY SCORE

Day 5

1. Circle the plural of ***emphasis***.
   emphases emphasises
2. Write the singular of ***fungi***. ______________
3. Rearrange the letters to make a word that means ***haven't remembered***.
   nfotgorte ______________
4. Write the homophone for ***waste***. ______________
5. The underlined word is a synonym ☐ or antonym ☐ for ***thrive***?
   win <u>flourish</u> fail melt
6. Expand the contraction in context. ______________
   She'd have to be the best runner in the school.
7. Adding the suffix ***able*** changes these
   v.______________ to n.______________.
   tolerate____ consider____
8. Punctuate the sentence.
   whale sharks found throughout the worlds tropical warm and temperate seas are the worlds biggest fish
9. Add speech marks to show what was said.
   Can people swim with whale sharks? I asked my mum.
10. Is the underlined word a verb ☐ or an adjective ☐?
    The <u>excited</u> tourists were looking forward to seeing the magnificent whale sharks.
11. Circle the verb group.
    You must not touch the animals or get too close.
12. Circle the noun that can't be touched.
    Everyone was watching out for a sign of the animals.
13. Write ***this*** or ***these***.
    Many whale sharks migrate to ______________ warm reefs between April and July each year.
14. Circle the pronoun and the noun it refers to.
    Tourists flock to the region so they can dive and snorkel with the giant whale sharks.
15. Circle the preposition.
    One enormous whale shark had a baby swimming next to it.

MY SCORE

Day 1

1. Rearrange the letters to make a word that means ***playful misconduct***.

   fimcheis ____________

2. ***serial*** or ***cereal***?

   Do you like to eat ____________ for breakfast?

3. Write the singular of ***leaves***. ____________

4. ***Whose*** or ***Who's***?

   ____________ bed does Goldilocks like the best?

5. Circle the simile.

   The bed she laid in first was as hard as stone.

6. The underlined word comes first in alphabetical order. Yes ☐ No ☐

   desire describe <u>delete</u>

7. Adding the suffix ***ness*** changes these

   adj____________ to n____________.

   lonely____ dark____

8. Circle the idiom (common expression).

   My dad has been working round the clock to perfect his cake recipe.

9. The underlined phrase is correct. Yes ☐ No ☐

   <u>Dad's recipe</u> Dads' recipe

10. Add speech marks to show what was said.

    This cake is absolute perfection! commented Mum after taking a bite.

11. Circle the verb group.

    She told Dad that he should enter the annual baking competion in town.

12. Circle the adverbs.

    Dad frequently bakes treats for our family and friends who gobble them up eagerly.

13. Rewrite in the simple past tense.

    Mum will buy the ingredients for Dad's new recipe.

    ____

14. Rewrite in the negative form.

    I help Dad with the baking.

    ____

15. Is the word ***reputation*** used correctly?

    Yes ☐ No ☐

    Dad baked the cake and put it in the reputation to cool.

MY SCORE

Day 2

1. Correct the spelling mistake. ____________

   We suffered through the swellterring heat on our holiday.

2. Write the homophone for ***higher***. ____________

3. Circle the plural of ***fungus***. funguss fungi

4. ***then*** or ***than***?

   I ate my meat and ____________ my vegetables because I like them better ____________ meat.

5. Complete the simile.

   As brave as a l____________.

6. Expand the contractions.

   1. ____________ 2. ____________

   After it's been in the oven, then it's ready to eat.

7. Add the prefix meaning ***external***.

   ____post ____side ____doors

8. Punctuate.

   the ancient aztec capital tenochtitlan is the present day site of mexico city

9. Add one or more apostrophes.

   It wasnt long before the population was drastically reduced due to foreign diseases.

10. Is the underlined word a verb ☐ or an adjective ☐?

    The Spanish colonisers <u>treated</u> the people of the Americas very badly.

11. Is the underlined word a verb ☐ or an adjective ☐?

    <u>Treated</u> wood is resistant to insects and fungal infestations.

12. Underline the proper adjectives.

    The Portuguese and Spanish conquistadores looted and ruthlessly destroyed the ancient cities.

13. Write the comparative or superlative form of ***large***.

    One of the ____________ temples still standing is in Coba, Mexico.

14. Circle the proper nouns.

    The leader of the Aztec civilisation, Montezuma II, was killed in a battle with the Spanish.

15. Circle the prepositions.

    Many things came from the Americas to the old world, including tomatoes, corn and chocolate.

MY SCORE

WEEK 32

Day 3

1. Rearrange the letters to make a word that means to ***trick or lie to someone***.

   ceivede ______________

2. ***bow*** or ***bough***?

   Do you need to ______________ when you meet the princess?

3. One salmon. Two ______________.

4. ***whose*** or ***who's***?

   Go and see ______________ at the door.

5. Complete the simile.

   As b______________ as a bee.

6. Which word comes directly after ***petite*** in alphabetical order?

   petal   petition   petty   pesticide

7. Adding the suffix ***able*** changes these

   v______________ to adj______________.

   adore_____   avoid_____

8. Circle the idiom (common expression).

   The jockey won the race by the skin of his teeth.

9. Which is correct?

   jockeys's horses   jockeys' horses

10. Add speech marks to show what was said.

    How does it feel to win the big race? the reporter asked the winning jockey.

11. Circle the sentence that needs speech marks.

    It was thrilling said the jockey.

    The jockey said it was thrilling.

12. Circle the abstract noun.

    Filled with pride, the winning jockey held up his trophy for everyone to see.

13. Circle the nouns.

    Next year, the jockey hopes to compete at Flemington with his winning horse.

14. Rewrite in the negative form.

    He will race again this week.

    ____

15. Is the word ***aimed*** used correctly?

    Yes ☐   No ☐

    The jockey aimed to win the race without getting injured.

MY SCORE

Day 4

1. Correct the spelling mistake. ______________

   You should always use your manners and be pollite to others.

2. Write the homophone for ***whole***. ______________

3. Circle the plural of ***hippopotamus***.

   hippopotamusses   hippopotami

4. ***then*** or ***than***?

   I liked the potato salad better ______________ the pasta salad.

5. Circle the simile.

   This steak is as soft as butter.

6. Expand the contractions.

   1. ______________   2. ______________

   I'd been sick all day, so I told my friend that I'd visit her tomorrow.

7. Add the prefix meaning ***between***.

   _____view   _____national

8. Punctuate the sentence.

   the disgusted children didnt want to eat boiled cabbage at lunchtime

9. The underlined phrase is correct. Yes ☐ No ☐

   <u>The child's cabbage.</u>   The childs' cabbage.

10. Circle the preposition.

    Fortunately, my mum was waiting for me at the office, so I didn't have to eat the cabbage.

11. ***advice*** or ***advise***?

    The cook will ______________ the children on how to eat the cabbage.

12. ***was*** or ***were***?

    One child ______________ sick before he ate the soggy cabbage.

13. Rewrite in the simple past tense.

    The cook will find a new recipe.

    ____

14. Circle the adjectives.

    The grateful children thanked their cook for taking the horrible cabbage away.

15. Circle the pronouns.

    'I will never cook cabbage again!' the relieved cook thought to himself.

MY SCORE

Day 5

1. Rearrange the letters to make a word that means ***from another country***.

   ngfrieo ________

2. ***fort*** or ***fought***?

   I once ________ a large bear in a dream I had.

3. Write the singular of ***breaths***. ________

4. ***Who's*** or ***Whose***?

   '________ book is this?' Dad enquired.

5. Complete the simile.

   As s________ as a fox.

6. Which word comes directly before ***overcast*** in alphabetical order?

   overdone   overact   overbearing

7. Adding the suffix ***ally*** changes these

   adj________ to adv________.

   dramatic____   frantic____

8. Circle the idiom (common expression).

   A beautiful diamond like this is only found once in a blue moon.

9. Which is correct?

   women's rings   womens' rings

10. Add speech marks to show what was said.

    How much does this sparkling, diamond ring cost? asked the wealthy lady.

11. ***she was*** or ***she had***?

    The lady told the jeweller that ________ seen the ring in the shop window.

12. ***isn't*** or ***aren't***?

    'A ring like that ________ cheap', the jeweller snapped rudely.

13. Circle the conjunction.

    The lady was offended by the shopkeepers comment, so she turned to leave the shop.

14. Rewrite in the negative form.

    You should be rude to paying customers.

    ____

15. Circle the prepositions.

    The wealthy lady went out the door and across the road to a different jewellery shop.

MY SCORE

Skill focus review

1. Correct the spelling mistake. ________

   There were four individules involved in the accident.

2. An antonym for ***turbulent*** is ________.

   crazy   choppy   calm

3. Expand the contraction in context. ________

   'Who's on the phone?' my dad asked me.

4. Add prefixes to make the words mean the opposite.

   ____agree   ____decided

5. The suffix ***able*** changes these words from

   v________ to adj________.

   avoid____   cure____   enjoy____

6. Circle the plural of ***cactus***.

   cactuss   cacti

7. Circle the idiom.

   Our new puppy is full of beans.

8. Punctuate the sentence.

   wolves can be found across north america northern europe and northern asia

9. Add one or more apostrophes.

   A wolf howls to communicate with its pack; wolves dont bark as often as dogs do.

10. Circle the proper adjective.

    The Arctic wolf is the only wolf species in the world with their unique white colouring.

11. Circle the masculine noun.

    A female and male wolf lead a wolf pack.

12. Circle the feminine noun.

    The alpha-female is the only wolf in the pack that is allowed to produce pups.

13. ***that*** or ***those***?

    The pack of wolves have left ________ large pawprints in the snow.

14. Circle the negative verb form and write as a contraction.

    ____

    The hungry wolf could not find any food.

15. Rewrite in the negative form.

    The wolf caught the rabbit.

    ____

WEEK 32

NOTES

NOTES

NOTES